TALKING WITH DONKEYS 4

RIDING FOR THE BRAND

MARK S. MEYERS

TALKING WITH DONKEYS 4

Since the year 2000, I have dedicated myself to one goal: **Build the best donkey rescue in the country.**

For all these many years I have ignored my health, neglected my family, alienated my friends and sacrificed my personal finances.

I didn't build the Peaceful Valley Donkey Rescue to gain fame for myself and I damn sure didn't do it for the money.

I did it because it was the right thing to do.

I did it because it needed doing.

I did it because sometimes you need to be a part of something bigger than yourself.

PVDR is my occupation, my passion, my religion, my obsession and most importantly: *MY BRAND*

In memory of my father.

Garold Dean Meyers
March 08, 1938 - April 19, 2012

This object that you are holding is not really a book. It may look like a book, feel like a book and even smell like a book, but it is not a book. Books are written by intelligent, educated authors. People that have dedicated themselves to the artistry of the written word.

This thing you are holding was written, photographed, and designed by a guy who rescues donkeys for a living. I am fluent in slang, profanity, redneck and I'm getting pretty good at Texan, but I ain't no wordsmith.

If you are offended by the corruption of the English language, you would be better served putting this one down and getting yourself another.

These are my stories, my memories and the philosophies that I live my life by. If you are cool with that, then by all means...Proceed!

Talking With Donkeys 4
Riding For The Brand

For information, contact:
Peaceful Valley Donkey Rescue, Inc.
PO Box 216 Miles, TX 76861
Phone 866-366-5731
www.donkeyrescue.org
info@donkeyrescue.org

Written by Mark S. Meyers
Book design by Mark S. Meyers
Photos by Mark S. Meyers & Amy L. Meyers
Cover photo by Troy Halfmann

ISBN: 978-0-9771471-8-2

Talking With Donkeys (TWD) Series
TWD: An Intimate look at the world's most maligned animals
Printed: August 01, 2005
TWD2: The simple philosophies of a 21st century burro man
Printed: June 01, 2006
TWD3: Saving them all
Printed: October 01, 2008
TWD4: Riding for the brand
Printed: February 25, 2013

This book is published by the Peaceful Valley Donkey Rescue (PVDR) in support of its work. Proceeds generated from the original sale of this book directly support the Rescue. No person has been compensated for their contributions.

This book represents the views, opinions and philosophies of Mark Meyers. If you are offended by any of its content please feel free to throw it away, give it to someone else or write your own damn book.

DEDICATION

To my dearest wife Amy. The first 20 years was one hell of a ride, can't wait to see what the next twenty bring.

July 18, 1992

FORWARD

Mark Meyers sells himself short as an author, while the prose is sometimes "uneven", that's to be expected: this book is a collection of short, dedicated sections, written at different times.

A "real" author would insist on revision after revision to "smooth" it out .. but that's unnecessary for the purpose of this book ... it's chock-full of information about PVDR and donkey-rescuing in general, great information on the animals themselves, and in particular, is a True Accounting of Mark Meyers, the man.

After being in close proximity to Mark for 14 straight months, I can attest (as was the case with Talking With Donkeys 3) that every word in this book is true.

He is who he is ...
and more importantly, he is who he says he is.

David Duncan
aka Doc Darlin

RIDING FOR THE BRAND

Table Of Contents

RIDING
FOR THE
BRAND

RIDING
FOR THE
BRAND

"Riding for the Brand means a lot of things:
Honor, loyalty, pride, trust. When you signed on with an outfit,
a "Brand", you were saying that you would put that Brand ahead
of yourself. You worked for it, you lived for it and you protected it
against any comers."

E. Watters
Professional Cowboy

THE DONKEY

As the whole focus of this book is on donkeys and their need for rescue, I thought it only fitting to begin with a little information about the species itself. Few people, other than donkey enthusiasts, know anything about these animals. So bear with me and see if you can't learn something.

don•key/dôNGkē/
Noun:
A domesticated hoofed mammal (Equus africanus asinus) of the horse family with long ears and a braying call; an ass.
A stupid or foolish person.

The American donkey is an ancestor of the original African Wild Ass. The African Ass was first domesticated around 4,000 BC in and around Egypt. Practical for its ability to learn quickly, carry heavy burdens and live on substandard feed, the African Ass quickly spread throughout the known world.

Donkeys were first introduced into the Americas over six hundred years ago by the early Spanish explorers. As a result of their work ethic and hardiness, they have become a common means of transportation and agricultural work in many of the poorer nations. Today, donkeys can be found in all countries of the Americas as well as most of the Caribbean Islands.

The common donkey has many uses. They can be used in agriculture in plowing and harvesting. They can transport heavy loads either on their back or by pulling carts. They can be ridden over long distances. Due to their protective nature, they can be used as guardians over flocks and herds, keeping predators at bay. Donkeys have a natural hatred of canines and are well known for defending against dog and coyote attacks. They have also been known to handle larger predators such as mountain lions.

Donkeys come in three general sizes based on their height at their withers (highest point of the back):

Miniature	36" or less
Standard	37"-55"
Mammoth	56" or greater

The terminology associated with donkeys is often confused. Here is a quick glossary of terms:

Jack	An intact male donkey
Jennet	A female Donkey
Gelding	A castrated male donkey
Foal	A young donkey
Burro	A wild, non-domestic ass
Mule	Hybrid cross between a jack donkey and a female horse
Hinny	Hybrid cross between a jennet don key and a male horse

The term "Donkey" is an old English word, combining "Dun" meaning gray and "Ky" meaning small. Dunkey or as now pronounced "Donkey" simply means a small gray animal. The word "Burro" is the Spanish word for donkey taken from the Latin "Burrisimo" meaning small horse. In the United States, we use the term "donkey" to describe the domestics or those living on a farm or ranch and "Burro" for those living in the wild.

Donkeys are extremely fast, with top speeds exceeding 30 miles per hour. An added benefit to the donkey's speed is its ability to watch all four feet while moving. This sure footedness was a tremendous asset to the donkey's use in packing and riding along precipitous trails in the Grand Canyon and similar areas. Donkeys are extremely hardy in inhospitable conditions. A donkey can survive four days without water and lose up to 30% of its body weight to dehydration without lingering effects. They can survive on the driest desert scrub brush, a diet that would kill a horse. The donkeys long ears act like a sail, catching the desert wind. This in turn cools the blood and helps regulate the donkey's internal temperature.

Wild burros in the United States are protected on lands administered by the Bureau of Land Management (BLM). In 1972, The Wild Horse and Burro Act was passed offering protection to these animals living wild in various states. As with all things political, this protection was subject to interpretation. Today, burros are considered feral pests and are being eradicated from public lands across the southwest on a Federal and State level.

Wild burro herds are generally segregated by sex. Large groups of jennets will group together to offer more protection for the young. These groups are matriarchal in nature and will be led by a dominate female. The young males are ejected from the herd at roughly 12 months of age. This helps to reduce the possibility of inbreeding. These jacks will move off on their own and stay in a loose groups known as a Bachelor Herd.

The Asian Ass (Equus hemionus) is a distant cousin to the African Ass. This species is extremely wild and has never been domesticated. Sometimes known as Onagers, this species is more horse-like and has a single stripe down the back and not the cross over the shoulders that is common in the African variety. The Asian Ass has five sub species:

Mongolian wild ass (khulan)
   Equus hemionus hemionus

Persian onager (gur)
   Equus hemionus onager

Indian wild ass (khur) Equus hemionus khur

Syrian wild ass,
   Equus hemionus hemippus (extinct)

Turkmenian kulan, (kulan)
   Equus hemionus kulan (pictured below)

These equids have been hunted for their pelts and for sport. The Syrian Wild Ass was hunted to extinction. Many of the other sub-species are endangered or very close to becoming endangered. The Turkmenian Kulan is a popular target at canned hunting ranches in the United States. Hunters often pay up to $10,000 for the opportunity to hunt one of these animals.

The many colors of donkeys

Red

Pink

White

Blue

Gray

Brown

Black

Brown Spotted

Gray Spotted

Black Spotted

Professor Jack's

"A tid bit of Knowlege"

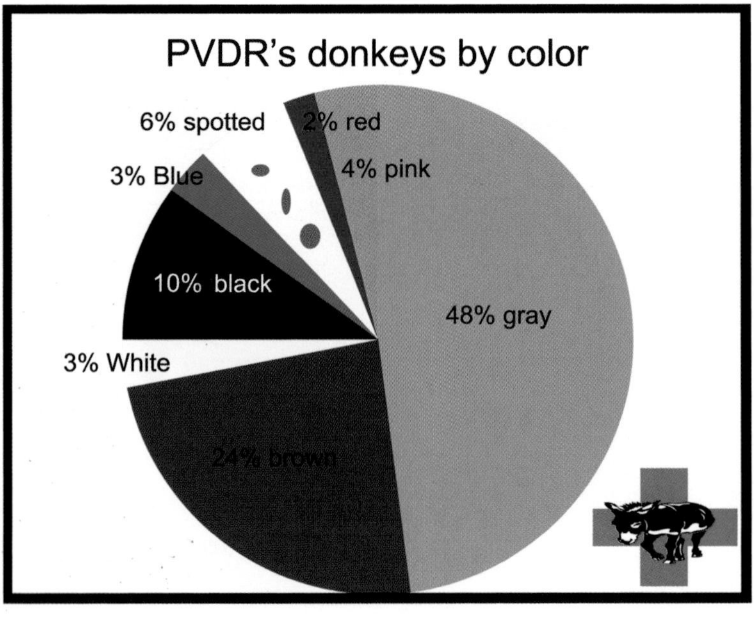

PVDR's donkeys by color

- 6% spotted
- 2% red
- 3% Blue
- 4% pink
- 10% black
- 48% gray
- 3% White
- 24% brown

I can run at speeds over 30 mph...

I can survive in the harshest climates...

I will not run from danger, but will confront it...

I can live four days without water and eat the barest desert scrub...

If you treat me kindly, I will be your most faithful friend...

What is so funny about being a jackass?
Peaceful Valley Donkey Rescue   www.donkeyrescue.org

THE NEED
FOR
DONKEY
RESCUE

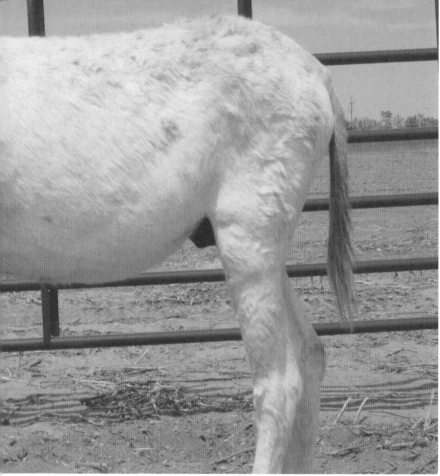

In the United States, donkeys are the butt of a long running joke. No one is really sure why this is... but it's true. In a poll sponsored by the Peaceful Valley Donkey Rescue, random people were asked to name three things about donkeys. Almost all responded: Stubborn, Stupid and Dangerous. We then asked if they had ever had actual contact with a donkey, not one of them had.

Where do these perceptions come from, if not from personal experience? Could it have something to do with Bugs Bunny or one of his pals briefly turning into a donkey when they did something foolish? Or maybe seeing Pinocchio turn into a donkey when he was over indulgent? No one thinks twice about calling someone a Jackass when they are being obstinate. Guilty without ever being charged. Donkeys have never had a chance, especially in our modern times.

But is this reputation deserved? If so, dedicating one's life to saving them from abuse, neglect and abandonment would seem a waste of time. Based on their obvious flaws, they probably had it coming. Right?

I have spent over a decade in the company of thousands of donkeys (to the tune of over 3,000 at publication). I can say, without a moment's hesitation, that donkeys are one of the smartest animals I have ever dealt with. They react and learn from experiences, not instinct. They are extremely difficult to trick as they are attentive to everything in their surroundings.

As for the stubbornness, perhaps the world is viewing that from the wrong perspective. A horse is trained from an early age to do whatever is expected of it without any thought for its own safety. Dogs are taught to immediately respond to commands, no questions asked. This is how we like our animals;compliant.

Now let us play a little game. I come by your place and say: "Hey let's go take us a walk over to the neighbors." And you say: "Why we gotta go to the neighbors?" And I say: "Cuz I told you to, dammit." and with that I grab a rope, tie it around your neck and start pulling you towards the neighbors. Now, in all honesty, what would your reaction be? Would you put you head down and meekly follow, or would you hit the brakes and say: "Now just a dog-gone minute!"

A donkey simply wants to feel comfortable in what is going on. Trust is a key factor and a donkey, that trusts you, will do whatever you ask, and yes, I said ask. I have asked donkeys to do all kinds of things, including walking down an almost vertical dry waterfall in Death Valley. They all did it, simply because they trusted me.

I was once loading a donkey into a trailer and this donkey was not cooperating. He didn't know me, he didn't know what a trailer was and he wasn't about to comply. An old man pulled up in a pickup truck and said: "That dumb SOB sure is stubborn, ain't he?" I just smiled and said: "Why don't you jump out of that truck and let me drag you in here? See how you like it?" He quickly rolled up his window and drove off, wonder if he got the point?

So, two out of three dispelled...but what about dangerous? I will admit to being kicked, bitten, stomped and dragged (all in a day's work in our profession). But in all these years and all of these confrontations, I was never surprised. A donkey will give you every opportunity to leave it alone, before it will resort to violence. It will move away, it will swish its tail, it will snort and if you still pester it, it may indeed become dangerous. But wouldn't most other animals?

TEXAS JACK'S

WORDS OF

WISDOM

THE MEASURE OF A MAN
IS FOUND IN THE WAY HE
TREATS WOMEN,
CHILDREN AND ANIMALS.

Unlike a horse's flight instinct, the donkey has a fight instinct. A donkey will not run away from danger, but will stay put and decide whether or not to engage. This helps them in their guardian tasks and makes them hard on unsuspecting dogs. I feel safer working with donkeys than I ever have around strange horses. Horses, especially wild ones, can be unpredictable. They will hurt themselves, and you, in their desperation to run from threat.

You: *"Come on Mark, all of these preconceived notions can't be completely unfounded."*

Me: *"Let me tell you a little story."*

Book of Numbers Chapter 22

This guy by the name of Balaam saddles up his donkey and heads off to do something or other. God gets plenty mad and sends a big scary angel to take Balaam out. The angel appears in front of Balaam and the donkey, but Balaam can't see him on account of he's all sideways with God. But the donkey can see him and turns away, saving Balaam. Balaam gets mad as a hornet and beats the donkey mercilessly and away they go again. But the angel is not done and appears again, donkey turns away, Balaam whips him.

Finally on a third attempt, the donkey has nowhere to turn so he simply lies down. Balaam completely loses control and just lets that donkey have it. While he is whipping the donkey, the donkey is given the power of speech and says: **"Why are you whipping me? Haven't I always been loyal? Haven't I always protected you?"**

And Old Balaam summed it all up by saying: **"Because you made me look stupid."**

Because of a donkey's ability to make its own decisions, it undermines our ability to have complete control. When you try and wrest that control away, you are often made to look stupid. And we all know that stupid people don't like to look stupid or as Mr. Gump put it: "Stupid is as stupid does".

Even with clearing up the misconceptions about donkeys, I still haven't addressed the bigger issue, the issue of whether or not they are worth saving. Our operation is massive and costly. Is our mission worth the expense?

Donkeys were originally brought to the Americas to work. They have participated in every aspect of our growing culture for more than 400 years. They built the missions, the roads, the railroads and they worked tirelessly in the mines. As modern inventions reduced their usefulness, they still found employment in tourism taking people down the Grand Canyon and as guardians of flocks.

The American Donkey represents our history as a nation of immigrants. The donkey has worked, sacrificed and endured to help build this country. Without his hardiness, our history would be written quite differently. And if this is true and the donkey is an important part of our history, isn't there a debt owed by those of us who benefit from it? Or do we turn a blind eye and say: "Sorry, your time has passed."

The Plight of the American Donkey rests on three problems that PVDR is working very hard to correct. Identifying these problems was easy, implementing their solutions...not so much.

#1: **Public Perception**
    As previously discussed, the general public has a predisposed, negative impression of the donkey. It is very difficult to solve these problems unless you are taken seriously. Given the opportunity I can usually convince people of the importance and the need for our work, but I have to get the opportunity first.

#2: **Abuse and Neglect**
    Not all people who neglect their animals are terrible people, some are just ignorant. They do not have access to the knowledge or cannot find someone to assist them. Many veterinarians and farriers (horseshoers) will not work on donkeys. Without anywhere to turn, the donkeys inevitably suffer. PVDR distributes thousands of Care and Feeding Manuals at no cost, all around the world. We also make a great deal of information available on our website:
www.donkeyrescue.org
and through our YouTube channel:
www.donkeyrescue.tv

#3: **Wild Burro Habitat**
    Hundreds of wild burros are either rounded up or shot to keep their numbers in check. There are many who feel that wild burro herds are being decimated as they compete for forage with cattle and have run afoul of the powerful cattle industry. PVDR works with many State and Federal Agencies in managing wild burro numbers. We strongly support sterilization and selective removal as opposed to outright decimation.

Internal and external parasite infestation along with malnutrition

Severe neglect leading to the front hooves curving like a ram's horns.

THE ORIGINS OF PEACEFUL VALLEY

The Peaceful Valley Donkey Rescue began as a backyard hobby on our little piece of property in Northern Los Angeles County. It was all very simple back then. Amy would find a donkey with an issue and we would fix it, more times than not, this was accomplished by simply spending my evenings sitting in the pen and talking with the donkey. We were doing well with our construction businesses, so money wasn't a huge factor, we continued this "find and fix" for several months until we had over 20 donkeys.

We realized early on that the two most important issues with animal rescue were money and room to house them. We knew that we would have to find homes for the donkeys, but also knew we couldn't just sell them. Selling an animal gives you no rights or say as to how the donkeys would be treated and what would happen to them, when the people didn't want them anymore. We needed a way to screen the homes, ensure proper care and ensure a safe future for them all.

We decided to start a non-profit corporation so that we could create an adoption policy and also to lend our little rescue a degree of legitimacy. The process to become a 501(c)(3) recognized organization is long and tedious. In December of 2000, PVDR became an entity unto itself.

All organizations need a name and we wanted a name that would work in any situation. We didn't want something too cute, we didn't want anything that could be made fun of and we didn't want a name that would ever limit us to a particular area. The property we lived on was on Peaceful Valley Road in Acton, CA and it just seemed to work. After all these many years, Peaceful Valley Donkey Rescue still works just fine.

We had no experience in the world of non-profits or animal rescue, so we ran it as we ran our regular business. We had customers (the donkeys). We offered services (transportation, medical, feed, etc.). We had vendors (Veterinarians, farriers, hay and feed suppliers). And we had partners (donors).

We approached the whole operation as a business. In order for any business to be successful you must have a set of guidelines from which you operate. PVDR's guidelines really haven't changed much since we began. We have matured in many ways but our business model is still pretty much the same.

In the beginning, we stuck to rescuing donkeys in our immediate area. There were enough to keep us pretty busy. Abuse and neglect were prevalent enough in our area, so we never seemed to be out of work. We realized early on, that in conjunction with rescuing donkeys, we had to educate owners to prevent future rescues from being necessary.

Our early success was given a huge boost from Animal Planet. We were lucky enough to be featured on various television shows as well as documentaries. This gave our fledgling organization the credibility to take the next step and expand our service area.

We began to get involved in wild burro capture and relocation in 2002. There are many wild burros throughout the western states and in many areas they are seen as destructive, the cheapest solution to reduce numbers is to shoot them. PVDR has been called into wild burro projects by Federal, State and Local agencies. We have provided assistance in the capture and transportation of hundreds of burros in four states.

Our reputation as a professional organization grew and with it came more and more requests for

Professor Jack's

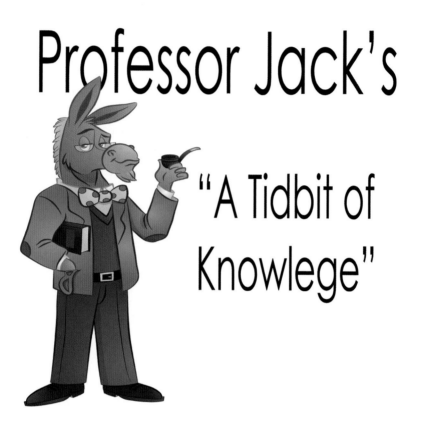

"A Tidbit of Knowlege"

Prior to the Texas drought PVDR rescued jacks and jennets in equal numbers, since the drought the ratio changed to 8 jacks to every two jennets.

help. Everywhere we looked, there were donkeys in desperate need of help. In order to keep up, we had to expand our adoption system to help move the donkeys into loving homes. Drinking coffee one morning and looking out over the donkeys, I had an epiphany... What if we find people to become mini-PVDRs? They would volunteer their time and facilities and operate under our rules, they adopt out our donkeys and they provide rescue services to their community. Unlike a charter or a chapter, our system was built on the premise that all of the Satellite Adoption Centers (SACs) were under the main office's direct control. PVDR made the rules, provided the donkeys and paid the expenses. This was a way that people could get involved in rescue work without the headache of the "business end" of being a charity. The satellite program has been a huge success with hundreds of donkeys being adopted in over 20 states.

Within a very short time, PVDR went from a community rescue to a nationwide organization. It became very apparent that we needed a more central location to facilitae and monitor our ever increasing organization. I moved to Texas in 2008 to establish a rescue and rehabilitation center. It was an ideal location as it was more centralized, offered cheap hay and had virtually no operational restrictions. Amy and my sons stayed to oversee our California operation and for the next two years I built Texas.

In 2009, we hired managers to handle the operations of the two rescue and rehabilitation ranches. It was our hope that by distributing some of the responsibilities, Amy and I could work on advancing the organization in other ways. Amy, Josh and Jake were finally able to join me in Texas in January 2010.

In late 2011, the rescue purchased an abandoned dairy in San Angelo, TX. This facility was ready made with large fenced paddocks, shelters, barns, work-shops and five water wells. As we were losing the lease on our current location, the timing could not have been better. With the help of some local high school boys, we were able to move our entire operation, including 800 donkeys, onto the new ranch in just over one week.

At the time of this printing, PVDR has decided to close our Tehachapi Rescue and Rehabilitation Center and consolidate all of our resources in San Angelo, TX. We have 17 Satellite Adoption Centers and provide rescue and adoption services in 32 states. We have well over 3,000 donkeys under our direct care on our ranches and sanctuaries.

Not too shabby for a back yard hobby.

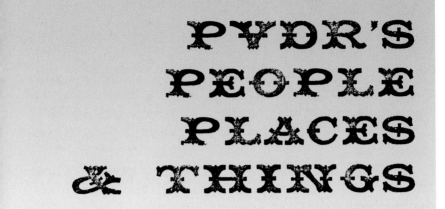

PVDR'S
PEOPLE
PLACES
& THINGS

By now, you are getting a clearer picture of the enormity of the Peaceful Valley Donkey Rescue. Rescuing, catching, transporting, feeding and caring for thousands of donkeys can be overwhelming. PVDR is nothing without the hard work of many dedicated people.

PVDR has a full-time staff of 5-7 people. These staffers handle everything from fundraising, administration, construction projects, maintenance and the care, feeding and rescuing of the donkeys. In all honesty, we could easily justify a full-time 10-12 people but to save money we all just work ridiculous hours. Most of us on staff work an average of 50 hours per week, some even more than that.

We employee 3-4 part-time staff as well. These are people that handle secretarial duties, ranch clean-up, ranch repairs and construction projects. Many of these positions are filled by high schoolers working on weekends. They are such a huge help and keep things going when the rest of us are busy with the donkeys.

The rest of the responsibility falls on the shoulder of our Satellite Adoption & Rescue Center volunteers. These dedicated men and women give their time and effort to not only place PVDR's donkeys into good homes but they also help to educate donkey owners, host PVDR fundraisers and information booths as well facilitate rescue cases in their areas.

Peaceful Valley also maintains a fleet of equipment in order to rescue and care for the many donkeys that we have. These pictures show some of the many things we do around here.

Mark Meyers Exec. Dir. / HMIC
Amy Meyers Chief Financial Officer

Zac Williams
Capture and Transport Specialist

David Duncan
Animal Nutrition Coordinator

Michele Halfmann
Administrative Assistant
Donkey Rescue TV Producer

Jake Meyers   Michael Tovar
Josh Meyers
Ranch Hands

Keeping up on the ranch requires 2 tractors.

Donkey Management System

Medical Bay

One of our transport rigs

Vicki MacKenney, pictured above, is PVDR's National Adoption Coordinator. Vicki and her husband Fred also operate our Satellite Adoption Center in Piedmont, OK.

The following pictures are of some of our other SAC Managers.

Satellite Adoption Center
Volunteer Program

Sandi & Tom White   Clermont, FL

Darlene & Joe Waldin   New Market, VA

Heidi Stump   Kent, IL

Mari & Marlin Spoonemore   Pollocksville, NC

Willis Walker   New Market, TN

Fred Clark & Joan Dunkle   Scenic, AZ

Kim Walker   Johnson, SC

Jim & Rhona Urquhart   Oregon City, OR
                Scott & Lura Shehan   Malvern, IA

Professor Jack's

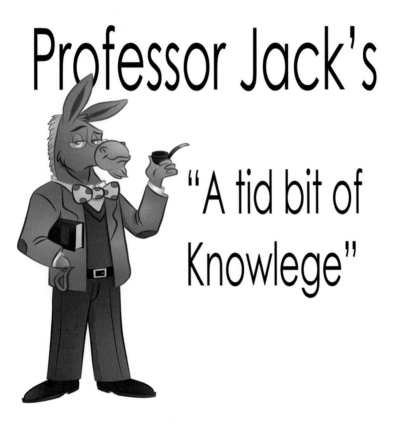

"A tid bit of Knowlege"

The Peaceful Valley Donkey Rescue has performed rescue work in 27 states and adopted donkeys in 23 states.

Bønney and I were featured on National Geograpic's website for our work during the Texas Drought.

Share

Photograph by Robb Kendrick

TEXAS

Since the drought started almost two years ago, Mark Meyers has taken in more than 800 donkeys at the Peaceful Valley Donkey Rescue, a shelter he and his wife, Amy, run near San Angelo, Texas. "With hay prices up to four times as much as usual, people could not afford to feed their donkeys," he says. "So they abandoned them." Meyers rounds up the strays with the help of Bonney and two other dogs.

www.robbkendrick.com

FAMILY LIFE

From The
Meyers
Oahu, HI
Oct. '07

Animal rescue, of any type, is all consuming. Regardless of the rescue's size, there is always more to do than a person has time to do it. As a result, many a marriage has fallen apart because of this time commitment. Unless both partners are totally committed, the strain eventually leads to a break. Fortunately for me, Amy is every bit as committed as I am.

Our marriage works well with PVDR. We work in the same office, we travel together as often as possible and we can be apart for extended periods without jealousy or resentment. I honestly believe that it is because of PVDR that we have a strong relationship, not despite it.

The Rescue has also been a great experience for my sons. Unlike my older children, Josh and Jake grew up with the Rescue. Work, donkeys, feeding, long hours, missed holidays are a part of every day life for them. They have learned that sacrifice and service is more important than selfishness and self pity.

Amy and I have always been very trusting of our sons. They have had to shoulder a huge responsibility from such a young age, that they have earned that trust. We never had a punishment system for them, even when they were young. In our world there simply is no excuse for not doing your job, so they always did their job. The only two rules that they have are that they have to take responsibility for their own actions and they have to always be respectful to their mother... you would be surprised how effective this is.

My older son Josh graduated second in his high school class. He is currently serving in the Texas National Guard and is attending Angelo State University near our home. Josh has aspirations of law school and Officer Candidate School in the Guard.

Jake, the youngest of my five children, is a drummer just like his old man. He has competed at the state level in individual solo competitions. Jake has joined the Texas National Guard and will ship off to Basic Combat Training in Fort Sill Oklahoma. Jake wll audition for the Army Band once his training is complete. Eventually Jake wants to open his own music store.

My three older children are all married and living in California. Shelly is mother to three wonderful kids Amaya Rae, Taya Naomi and Teijo Mark.

My eldest, Sherae, is a comedian by trade and has a daughter named Ivy Pearl.

MY
BELIEFS

I think beliefs are great. I think that they reassure people, give them hope and a promise of things to come. The trouble with me is...I don't have any. I am a non-believer in all aspects of the word. If I can't see it, touch it, feel it, taste it...it doesn't exist, and I'm totally okay with that.

The reason I felt compelled to include this chapter in the book is simple: If I do not believe in a heaven or a rainbow bridge, then when I put an animal down, I know that it is over.

I am saying that "nothingness" is better than what this donkey is going through right now. To me, it puts things into a clearer perspective. If I thought for a second that the donkey would wake up in green fields with pretty flowers, I would not hesitate to put it out of its misery.

I also think that the notion of an animal heaven alleviates a little too much guilt from the people responsible for the animal's fate. Let's say I don't want the hassle of my dog any more. I drop it off at the pound, they give it the gas and I walk away with the comforting knowledge that little Scruffy is in heaven.

Death is forever and it is not a decision to be taken lightly. Before we euthanize a donkey, we take several things into consideration. Can the donkey be medically treated to save its life? Sometimes the treatment is simply too costly and we cannot afford it. In truth, PVDR does not have any $10,000 donkeys. We simply can't. We must be practical in our decisions.

Can the donkey get up and around on its own? Can it stay up for awhile if given assistance? Is it in constant pain? Can it eat, drink and relive itself under its own power? Do we have a reasonable expectation

There is an old Indian legend that says when a man dies he must cross a bridge into the afterlife. At the head of this bridge waits every animal that he encountered during his lifetime. The animals decide which of us can cross and which are turned away.

that the donkey may recover? Can it socialize with other donkeys?

These are tough decisions to make, but as the caretakers, it is our responsibility.

I have great respect for people of all religions and faiths. I have an even greater respect for those who don't try and force their beliefs on me. I am a firm believer in the saying, "You be you and I'll be me".

All too often, people will allow their beliefs to infringe on the lives of others. We all do not have to agree on where we came from or where we are going, but I do not see a future in a planet that is constantly fighting over whose version of the truth is the right one. Chopping people's heads off, picketing at soldiers funerals and telling gay people who they can and cannot marry, all these things are being done in the name of a God who is supposed to be loving, peaceful and merciful, just sayin'...

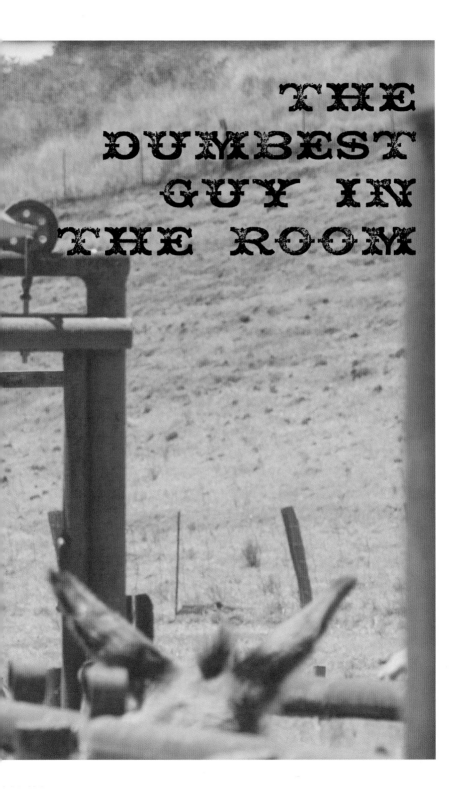

THE
DUMBEST
GUY IN
THE ROOM

I think that my extreme lack of education has been a good thing when it's comes to PVDR. I never learned how others "did it". I never learned what "never worked". And probably the most important lesson I never learned was "how to think out of the box". What does that even mean? To "think outside of the box" you have to know what it means to think "inside the box". But...if you don't know what the box is, you are always on the outside.

Seriously, the worst thing that can happen is that you reinvent the wheel and what's so bad about that? You look around and say "No shit, you guys figured out the whole wheel thing, too?"

I did very well in school. I graduated in the top 3% of my high school and my college prospects were good. The only problem was that I REALLY DIDN'T WANT TO GO!

At 18 years old, I was absolutely convinced that I was going to be a rock star drummer. What in the hell would a rock star drummer need with a college degree? (don't answer that, it was rhetorical).

So while I banged on the drums, I supported myself as an electrician. It was honest work, and paid a decent enough wage that we did not starve. As I advanced through the ranks of my field, I eventually became my own boss, with my own company and more than a fair chunk of the American dream.

My education did not come from a classroom, but from J.B. Wise. J.B. was my mentor and taught me more about business and work ethic than I could have ever achieved in a school. Like me, J.B. did not attend college but learned from a mentor as well. The rules he taught were practical, they were real life and they held real consequences. In business, every decision is judged by its profitability and losing money is not an option. My education under J.B. lasted for four years and every minute was invaluable. My mother often asks if I regret not going to college and truth be told, I don't. My life's path has had many twists and turns in it, some really good and some really, really bad. But if I were to have gone to college, someone else would be writing this book about donkeys and I would be somewhere else. I like how it has all turned out...nope wouldn't change a thing.

Now don't get me wrong: A COLLEGE EDUCATION IS IMPORTANT.

My attorneys have a college education. My accountants have a college education. My veterinarians have a college education. My urologist has a college education. And I am glad that I can pick up the phone and have the full benefit of their knowledge and expertise.

I just don't think that college is for everyone. I came up in the "trades". I never once felt like I was less than everyone else because I worked with my hands. This country was built by trades people and somehow we have fallen away from that. Pushing kids to go to college is OK, but what if they are really dumb? What if they have a natural talent or interest elsewhere?

But I digress...back to me

PVDR is what it is because of me. My force of personality, my intelligence, my strength of character and my brass balls. If you have read this far into the book you now realize just how big PVDR is. We are like no other rescue in size or scope. We have done more

Burroman says

"It's OK to be a redneck"

RECIPE FOR "TWINE"
(REDNECK ICE TEA)

1/2 FULL GALLON SIZE JUG OF
UNSWEET ICE TEA

FILL THE OTHER HALF OF THE JUG
WITH RED BOX WINE.

SHAKE WELL & ENJOY!

for a single species than any other rescue had accomplished in the history of our country and all because I didn't know any better and would not take NO for an answer.

Many times over the last 12 years I have run into obstacles. Whether it was government agencies, insurance companies or financial institutions I have always heard "You can't do that", "That's not how so and so did it", "That has never been done before." Well guess what? There is a new sheriff in town and we are going to do it, with you or without you. I have always tried to play by the rules but if the rules prevent PVDR from fulfilling its mission, then the rules gotta go.

I guess it all comes down to this: You can accomplish anything as long as no one tells you otherwise. Shakepeare never studied Shakespeare. Many highly successful movie directors not only didn't go to film school, they never graduated high school. Success comes from equal parts creartivity and tenacity.

So being the dumbest guy in the room has never bothered me. In fact: I think it worked out just fine...

MAKING A DIFFERENCE

In the summer of 2012, we decided to close our California Facility. The decision was a long time coming. There was a long list of reasons to close it: hay was too expensive, insurance requirements were ridiculous, the ever-intrusive state, county and local governments and the donkey-hating neighbors are but a few.

The thing that capped it really came down to two things: In 2011 PVDR-TX performed over 700 rescues while PVDR-CA only did 7, but the main reason was...It is just too hard to find good help. Try as we might, we could not find anybody that could work unsupervised, would actually show up and who wasn't a complete nut ball.

When I finally convinced the Trustees that the time was right, I then had to begin the process of relocating everything. Zac was holding down the fort in Texas and trying to keep up with the rescues, as well as the sanctuaries, so I was the one that had to handle California. For six solid months, I was on the road four out of every six days. A round trip from San Angelo, Texas to Tehachapi, California is 2,600 miles and takes 40 driving hours.

There were over 450 donkeys to be moved, but not just moved. We had to build the proper facilities to handle some of the special needs donkeys. These included our Domestic Seniors, Wild Seniors, Hoof and Leg Pen and Mules. There were also the livestock to consider:

3 Cows   8 Goats   3 Sheep   7 Pigs   4 Geese

And once all of that was done, I had to start moving the equipment. We had miles of pipe corral, shelters, buildings, feed troughs, chutes, alleys and the list goes on. It was cheaper to transport these items than to re-purchase them in Texas. PVDR-TX is a great facility but with the addition of so many new herd groups, we needed everything we owned.

Once the new donkeys were settled in, I had to show the Texas staff who was who. Some of the donkeys that had been relocated from California are on the Permanent Resident List. As we were walking through the lots I was pointing out different ones and giving their names and stories.

There was Izzy our very first donkey. There was Deuce, the second wild burro I had ever caught. Snoopy from the first Sheldon Project. Jed and Waylon from one of our first rescue cases. Parker, a wild burro with a broken hip that we caught near Parker Arizona and the list went on. Some are permanent because they are extra special to us, others because they have an issue that makes them un-adoptable. As I was reminiscing, I realized why I knew all of these donkeys and could remember their stories. In the early years we would only rescue one or two at a time. Each case

was special and it meant something.

Now, we seldom go on a rescue run unless we can get at least 20 donkeys. With so many donkeys needing our help, we have to be as efficient as possible. Unfortunately, when you bring in 20 donkeys from four different counties the stories and faces all kind of blur together. In many ways, I miss the old days. Things were much simpler back then. I had a lot more time to just talk with donkeys and hang out.

I did an interview in 2004 for the Los Angeles Times. In the interview the reporter asked if I thought I was making a difference and without hesitation I said "no". Yes, we had made a difference to the ones that we had rescued, but we hadn't put a dent in the real problem. Eight years later I would answer that question totally different. Not only are we making a real difference, we are doing it without much help.

Peaceful Valley Donkey Rescue is my life. I have lived, breathed, bled and fought for it for over twelve years. I am proud of it and what it has accomplished but the price for success was very steep. I have lived away from my family for months at a time. I have ignored my health and I have worn myself out. The reason no one else can make these claims of success that we can is because no other group of people were willing to sacrifice all.

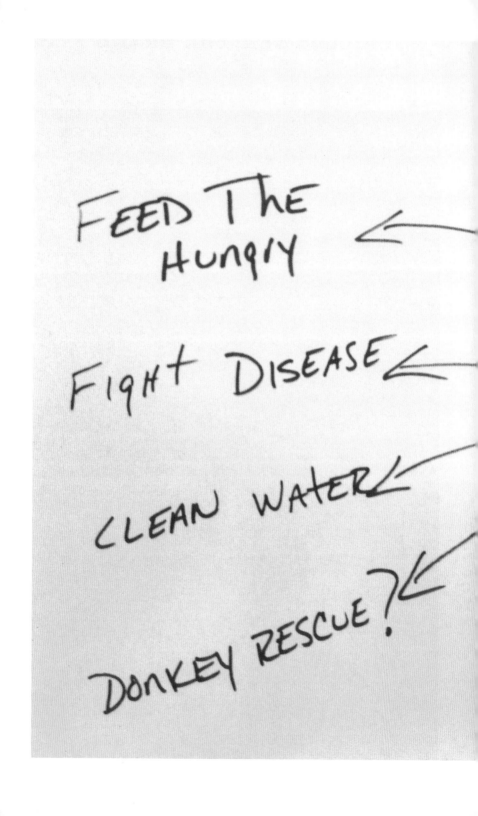

PUBLIC
BENEFIT

One thing that many skeptics of donkey rescue will ask is: "How is rescuing donkeys a benefit to the public?"

I think this is a very fair question to ask. In the big picture we, the non-profit sector, are a drain on the tax base. Donations that go to charities lower the amount of taxes collected by the government. The reason this system came about was so that the non-profit sector could take on many of the responsibilities that would otherwise fall to the government. Another benefit of this system is that the work of non-profits is supported only by people that have an interest in the work performed. But...it has to be a benefit to the public.

The act of rescuing a donkey is not a benefit to any one except the donkey. This isn't confined to just donkeys; dogs, cats, horses, hamsters it's all the same. "Where is the public benefit?"

PVDR is a public benefit on many levels. The biggest benefit is our work with law enforcement. Many county sheriff departments are responsible for the collection and management of stray animals. In some of the more affluent counties, there may be a separate county office, but especially in Texas this responsibility falls to the Sheriff.

Many states have Estray Laws that govern the handling of stray animals. In Texas, the Estray Laws call for the holding of the animals for up to 21 days while advertisements seek the owners. If the owners claim the animals, they usually pay a boarding fee that compensates the county. If the owners cannot be found, the animals are sold at auction and the money received is used as reimbursement for the sheriff department's expenses. These Estray Laws were written long ago based on the concept that the animals had financial value. In Texas, donkeys hold no financial value so they cannot be sold. The Sheriff Departments are stuck paying between $5.00 to $10.00 per day boarding fee per donkey and the counties just cannot afford this.

The Sheriff Departments find themselves in the same position as John Q. Public, they cannot sell, trade or even give away the donkeys in their possession. As the boarding fees continue to mount, the Sheriff must make a real decision between paying for deputies and paying for the donkeys. Some Sheriffs have actually brought the donkeys to their personal ranches to help defray the costs. Without PVDR's assistance, these departments and these donkeys would be in dire straights.

Another public benefit we provide is the assistance to the Federal Government. PVDR works with the Bureau of Land Management (BLM), National Park Service (NPS), U.S. Fish and Wildlife Service(USFWS) and the U.S. Department of Agriculture (USDA). Some of the larger projects Include:

200+ BLM Wild Burros
Ridgecrest, CA Palomino Valley, NV Kingman, AZ

In 2007, Congress passed a law mandating that the BLM must sell any horse or burro over 10 years old. Typically horses and burros captured by the BLM were put up for adoption or held at one of their facilities. As many people were not interested in older horses, the inventory kept growing increasing the feed costs. The law meant that the "sale" animals were no longer protected by the Wild Horse and Burro Act of 1971. To ensure the safety of the these burros, PVDR has taken in the majority of them.

250+ USFWS Wild Burros
Sheldon Antelope Refuge, NW Nevada

The Sheldon Antelope Refuge is home to a large wild horse and burro population. These animals are not protected under the Wild Horse and Burro Act as these lands are not managed by the BLM. PVDR has been involved with this project since 2004 and have captured and/or transported nearly 300 wild burros since that time.

60+ USDAWild Burros & Domestic Donkeys
Presidio, TX

Burros, both wild and domestic, wander back and forth across the Rio Grande river along our border with Mexico. These burros are often caught by the USDA Wrangler or in one of the traps we have set up in this region. Many of these burros are part of the herd known as The Big Bend Burros. These burros were made famous because Texas Parks and Wildlife has shot over 100 of them.

1000+ Texas Domestic Donkeys

Due to the extreme 2010 drought in Texas, donkey abandonment became a huge issue. Donkeys were being abandoned by the hundreds. PVDR led the way in assisting the county law enforcement agencies. In many cases, PVDR was required to capture these donkeys on vast tracts of land.

PAYING
FOR
PVDR

It is nearly impossible to raise money for donkeys without giving an explanation. Don't believe me? Try this...

Walk into any bar in the United States and say, "We are passing the hat for hungry kids", "For breast cancer", "For the whales." People will either give or not, but they will automatically know what you are talking about.

Now walk back in and say, "We are passing the hat for donkeys". After the initial laughter dies down, you get to try and explain why donkeys need help. There are not donkey supporters lurking behind every tree and we have to look far and wide to find people that are interested enough to even allow us to explain.

Give me fifteen minutes of your time and I'll make a donkey lover out of you. I will tell you stories about mistreatment, about awful neglect, despicable abandonment and loss of habitat. Give me the chance and I can tell you why donkeys not only need your support but deserve your support. But...I always have to explain.

I attended the Fund Raising School at Indiana University's campus in Indianapolis. At these classes I met fundraisers from the Salvation Army, Girl Scouts, and the United Way as well as representatives of major universities. In every class I was voted the guy with the toughest job. Their causes were all "automatic". Their perspective donors knew about their cause and either felt a connection to give or they didn't, but they at least had an immediate opinion. With donkeys, nothing is automatic. It has to be earned, one supporter at a time.

Professor Jack's

"A tid bit of Knowlege"

The vast majority of PVDR's financial support comes from the West Coast and East Coast. Texas uses 90% of PVDR's rescue resources but only contributes 5% of its income.

Most of our support comes from direct mail letters sent through the post office. I write a letter about a donkey that we have rescued and I try very hard to get you to open it. If it makes it past the junk mail pile and you actually read it, I have a pretty good chance that you will become a donkey supporter.

Another difficulty in raising money for donkeys is in the stigma. No one wants to have their name, personal or corporate, associated with a "jackass". Corporations can easily advertise their support and involvement with many of the common charities, but would have to include an explanation of their support of us. It is just easier not to.

Political involvement is also another problem. Many of our ranches and by default our events are located in conservative districts. This is not by any design, but rural areas usually trend towards Republican. As the donkey is the symbol of the Democrat party, it would be political suicide to chance having a picture with a donkey in it. So we are unable to attract any high profile people to help rally our cause.

This stigma reaches even to celebrities. We have asked, pleaded and begged for a nod or kind word from a celebrity and have always come up empty. The only interest was from people that wanted to make fun of the donkeys or do something stupid with them. As this would be counterproductive to our cause, we rely on regular people...much like you!

THE PVDR PROCESS

Peaceful Valley Donkey Rescue is an enormous organization with a reach that extends from Coast to Coast, Border to Border and even to Hawaii. We have the capabilities of rescuing donkeys from anywhere in the United States within a matter of days. This even includes the ability to rescue large numbers of donkeys, 100+, from dire situations at the same time. From wild burro captures to law enforcement seizures, PVDR is unequalled.

The hard part to all of this is not the rescuing of donkeys but rather the care of the donkeys once they are in our system. Dealing with thousands of donkeys would be overwhelming if not for our system that we have designed and implemented since our earliest days. Here is how it works:

A Rescue Case is created on our website at www.donkeysurrender.org. All of the pertinent information regarding the case is recorded and forwarded to our Surrender Coordinator and the case is issued a rescue case number for easy tracking.

The Rescue Coordinator reviews the information and determines if help is available and if so how soon should help be sent. Not all rescue cases are approved for involvement by PVDR. Many people simply grow tired of their donkeys and want to dump the responsibility onto us. We cannot take these donkeys as they would take the space that is needed by donkeys in real peril.

PVDR also will not buy donkeys from an auction. A donkey at auction is not necessarily in peril. Any information that might indicate that the donkey is in peril would come from the individual selling the donkey who also has the most to gain from the donkey's sale. We have a limited amount of resources and must use these resources to rescue the donkeys that need us the most. Once a Rescue Case has been cleared for action, a decision must be made as to the time frame we have to get to the donkey. Many donkeys come to us from law enforcement agency seizures or captures. These donkeys typically are in a holding facility and can wait until we can schedule a trip in an area where we can do many pickups in the same day. Others such as severe neglect and abuse might need to be picked up the very same day as the case is recorded. Each Rescue Case is unique and must be addressed on an individual basis. Sometimes nothing more than backing up a trailer to a loading chute is needed but other times a trap must be set up and the BurroCollies must be called in to catch the donkeys on large tracts of land. Irregardless of the scenario, PVDR must respond in a timely and professional manner, always.

Upon arrival at one of PVDR's Rescue and Rehabilitation Facilities, the donkeys are placed in our quarantine area. All donkeys, regardless of origin, must spend a minimum of three weeks under supervised quarantine. If after the three week period the donkeys are healthy in all aspects they move into processing.

Processing a donkey into our system is one of the most important parts of the donkeys transition into the PVDR system. The donkeys are checked for overall health including body mass, teeth, hooves and joints. Their age and sex is recorded and they are given a broad spectrum vaccine and a deworming agent. The final step is to insert a microchip under the skin of their neck to identify that donkey for life.

All of the information gathered during processing is recorded into our custom made data system. In

DonkeyId 2053346481

Name	Izzy	AVID	085-070-364
Last #	364	DOB	03/01/99
Received In	06/01/00	Received From	Owner Surrender
Desig	Domestic Donkey	Color	Brown
Sex	Jennet	Castration	
BLM		Blm #	
Origin City	San Diego	Origin State	CA
Status	Permanent	Rescue Case ID	20,000,600

Picture One

Care Records

	Created	Type	Facility	Person	Note
📝	11/27/11	Care	TXHA	Texas Ranch	
📝	03/12/09	Care	TXMI	Former Texas Ranch	
📝	03/11/05	Care	CATE	California Ranch	
📝	06/01/00	Care	CAAC	Mark & Amy Meyers	

Medical Case

2008, we contracted with a company called Lightspoke (www.lightspoke.com) to build a comprehensive, state of the art, Internet based data system. This system is AWESOME!

Every donkey has its own "Donkey 360" which is an individual file and contains:

Microchip number:
Date of birth:
Date received:
Sex: Jennet, Jack or Gelding
Date of castration: (once performed)
Designation: Domestic Donkey or Wild Burro
Rescue Case Number:
Received from: Captured, Government Agency, Bureau of Land Management, Born at PVDR, Rescue surrender, Owner surrender, Stray
Origin City:
Origin State:
Height: Mini, Small standard, standard, large standard, mammoth
Status: Available, Not available, Permanent, Adopted, Medical hold, Sanctuary, Deceased
And two uploaded pictures

Attached to each Donkey 360 are searchable modules:

Medical records: Tracks all medical ailments and procedures performed on the donkey while in our care.
Care Records: Tracks the donkey's location within the PVDR system

Notes: Additional information such as "Bad with dogs", "Trained to Drive" etc.

All rescue cases and adoption applications are also uploaded to Lightspoke via our website so that these files are also attached to the donkey. Giving us a complete start to finish history, like I said: **AWESOME!**

Once processed and inputted into our system, we must make a decision on where to place the donkey. The donkey's age, health and temperament are evaluated and then the donkey is placed into either:

Ranch Herds: Seniors, Pregnant jennets, Jennets, Jacks, Senior jacks, Geldings and Weanlings

Sanctuary: Those donkeys that do not display friendliness or are having issues adjusting to domestic life.

Adoption: Donkeys that are friendly, will accept a halter and will allow all four hooves to be trimmed

TEXAS JACK'S

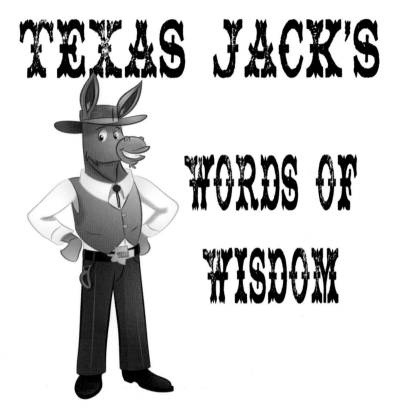

WORDS OF

WISDOM

WHEN YOU GIVE A
PERSONAL LESSON IN
MEANNESS TO A CRITTER
OR A PERSON, DON'T BE
SUPRISED IF THEY LEARN
THEIR LESSON.

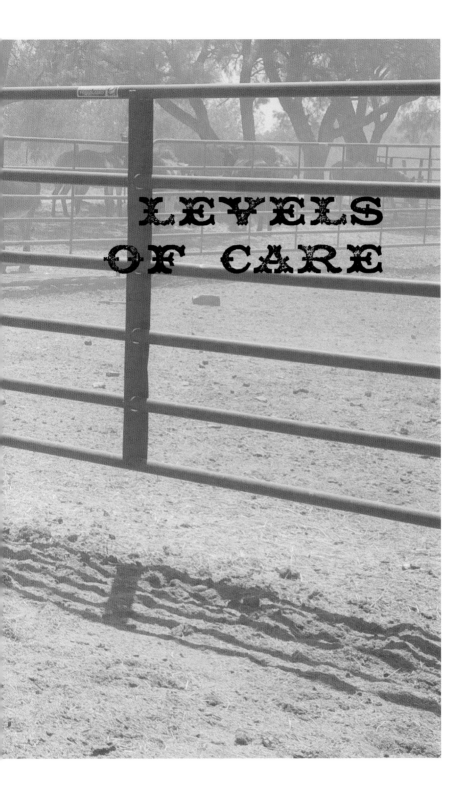

LEVELS OF CARE

Care Level 1
Seniors & Hoof Cases
Approximate monthly cost per donkey $125.00
Temperature controlled shelter
Special feed and nutritional supplements
Medicines and/or medical supplements
Modified worming and vaccines
Daily medical checks
Weekly/Biweekly veterinary evaluations

Care Level 2
Holding pens, various medical issues
Approximate monthly cost per donkey $100.00
Fully enclosed shelter
Special feed and nutritional supplements
Medicines and/or medical supplements
Modified worming and vaccines
Daily medical checks
Monthly veterinary evaluation

Care Level 3
Quarantine
Approximate monthly cost per donkey $65.00
Individual Shelter
Special feed and nutritional supplements
Medicines and/or medical supplements
Modified worming and vaccines
Daily medical checks
Initial veterinary evaluation then as needed basis

Care Level 4
Pregnant and Nursing Jennets
Approximate monthly cost per donkey $65.00
Group Shelter
Grass hay with grain supplement as needed
Standard worming and vaccines
Weekly medical checks
Veterinary evaluation as needed

Care Level 5
Standard herds
Approximate monthly cost per donkey $40.00
Group Shelter
Grass hay diet
Standard worming and vaccines
Weekly medical checks
Veterinary evaluation as needed

Care Level 6
Sanctuary
Approximate monthly cost per donkey $20.00
Natural shelter
Pasture and natural forage
Standard worming and vaccines
Weekly observation
3- month medical checks
Veterinary evaluation as needed.

WWW.DONKEYRESCUE.TV

KEEPING UP WITH THE TIMES

Technology, and everything that the term encompasses, moves faster than I am able to keep up with. It seems like by the time I figure out the latest and greatest, it is already outdated. At PVDR, we have done our best to stay current and get the most out of what technology has to offer.

Websites

Our website is the highest placed URL on any search engine. That means that if you searched for "donkey rescue", www.donkeyrescue.org would be at the top of the list. We are very proud of this and have worked hard to earn this spot.

Our website allows visitors to learn about donkeys, explore our rescue services, make a donation, support a particular rescue project, sponsor a donkey, shop our gift store, submit an adoption application and submit a rescue case.

In 2012, we added a mobile site for smart phone users. www.donkeyrescue.mobi is a great way to attract people who see our trucks on the road. By texting "donkey" to 72727, they will receive a short text describing our work and a link to the mobile site. While not as extensive as our regular site, there are many things to explore.

Lightspoke

In 2008, PVDR contracted with a company to build a web based data system that would track all of the donkeys under our care. Lightspoke.com came through big time. This data system allows us to keep track of all Active, Completed and Suspended rescue cases. PVDR receives 8-12 new cases every week, so tracking and organizing them is critical.

The system allows us to create an individual file for every donkey. It tracks all of the donkeys personal information: AVID number, name, date of birth, date received in, color, sex, rescue case number, wild or domestic and the reason for rescue. This information is then placed "in care of" a Rescue and Rehabilitation facility, a Satellite Adoption Center, a Sanctuary or an Adoptive Home. This means that we can search for any donkey and know exactly where that donkey is currently located. This system also tracks all medical treatments that have been performed on the donkey.

Social Media
We have always strived to use social media to our advantage. As a free form of advertising, Facebook, Pinterest and Twitter, the current most common forms of social media, have been very helpful in raising awareness and funds for the rescue.
www.twitter.com/donkeyrescue
www.facebook.com/peacefulvalleydonkeyrescue
www.pinterest.com/donkeyrescue

Donkey Rescue TV
In 2012, PVDR launched a YouTube channel called Donkey Rescue TV. In our channel, visitors can watch videos of the donkeys at play, learn different techniques employed by PVDR staff and see the BürroCøllies in action.
www.donkeyrescue.tv
www.youtube.com/donkeyrescuetv

PVDR
ETHOS

We have an Ethos here at PVDR, one that was instilled in me at a company that I once worked for and later owned. It was really a simple ideology: You are either an hourly man or an oath man. An hourly man is one who trades his hours for money. The balance comes from his production versus the amount of financial compensation. The relationship extends no further than this balance. As most hourly men feel they are under paid, there is a tendency to produce less in an effort to "balance" the scale. The employer on the other hand feels that since the hourly man agreed to the terms of the arrangements, his production should remain constant. These relationships are doomed to failure and hourly men usually end up wearing a different color apron at their new hourly job within a few months.

An oath man is one that accepts the company's Ethos or set of guiding beliefs. In my early years as an electrician, I was an hourly man. I traded my time for a paycheck at the end of the week. I never stayed late, unless paid overtime. I worked my hours and cashed my check. The scales were balanced...and I never, ever got ahead.

In 1988 I hired on with a company called Wise Electric, that was building a regional shopping mall. There were 220 electricians on this project and I made 221. After settling into my working environment, I noticed a group of men within the company. These were not necessarily the foreman, or supervisors but some were just regular old electricians like me but somehow they were different. They were known as the Wise Guys.

The Wise Guys were set apart from the rest of us by their actions, not their words. They never discussed their little club, but we all knew it existed. They were the ones that were already on the job when the rest of us arrived in the morning. They were the ones "finishing up a few things" when it was time to leave for the day. And most importantly, they were the ones who made sure that everyone followed the rules and never bad mouthed the boss or the company. In short, they were scary.

After several months of proving my electrical prowess, I was approached by the boss himself, Mr. J.B. Wise. J.B, as I was later allowed to call him, took me for a walk around the project and explained the relationship between employee and employer, much as I am doing to you right now. He explained that as long as I produced the expected amount of work, he would produce the agreed to amount of money. He went on to explain that he had heard promising things about me, but as long as we were governed by a dollar to hour relationship then I would be just another employee. As we ended our talk, J.B. shook my hand and said, "Have you ever considered being worth more than your paycheck?" and with that he turned and walked away.

The time I had spent talking to J.B. cut my day short and I still had some work to do in order to finish the project that I was working on. Instead of quitting on time, as was my normal, I decided to stay a little

late and finish up. I was immediately surrounded by Wise Guys who leant me a hand and helped me finish the task in just a few minutes. The next morning, I arrived early and helped a few guys on their task prior to starting my day. I won't bore you with the details, but years later I owned Wise Electric and found myself having the exact same conversation with my own new employees that J.B. had with me, so many years ago.

By simply putting the well being of the company ahead of my own interests, the company prospered. The more the company prospered, the more money, benefits and respect I earned. By placing the company ahead of myself, I became a part of something. I had others that I could count on and in turn counted on me. I had a code of conduct that set me apart from others. And I had a sense of pride in what the company was able to accomplish.

The beliefs, that we swore to back then, are the same as those that I follow with PVDR today. PVDR still has hourly men (and women), but we also have oath men, and that is why we are successful.

The PVDR Ethos:

*Place the interests of PVDR
ahead of your own*

Protect PVDR's imagine

Keep PVDR's secrets

Defend PVDR's honor

BUYING YOUR BEST

Almost every Peaceful Valley Donkey Rescue employee, at one time or another, has walked into my office to scold me. Every single one, and they all say the same thing. "How come you never tell me when I'm doing something right, but when I'm doing something wrong you get on me right away?"

You would think that after all of these years of being asked this question, I might change my ways. Maybe start slapping backs and giving 'Atta-Boys'. I am sure I could google hundreds of tips on employee management. I could even learn to use some of those goofy "office speak" words like "reach out to", "expedite" and "circle back to", but that just ain't going to happen.

My response to these "team members" or "associates" is always the same. I thought I was buying a good job. When I negotiate a wage with an employee, I am agreeing to pay a certain amount of money in exchange for a good job. I am not paying for a mediocre job so that I can praise you when you do something right and chastise you for doing something wrong.

In my way of thinking, atta-boys are for children playing T-ball and dogs learning a new trick. as adults, shouldn't we know that we are expected to perform at our best? Advancement comes (or at least it should come) from effort and performance, not from time served. As an employer for over 20 years, I notice the better workers, the ones making the effort. I also notice the dullards, the ones that are just marking time and collecting a paycheck. I promote employees based on their performance and not their seniority.

I admit that I give praise sparingly. J.B. used to say, "I just want to see the baby, I don't want to hear the labor pains.". So many employees want their boss

to know just how difficult the assigned task was. How much blood, sweat and tears were shed. How many late nights and personal sacrifice....you get the picture.

Any good boss worth his salt can do the job of his subordinates. There is no facet of donkey rescue that I have not done. I have shoveled, raked, dragged, lifted and tractored. I have unrolled, stretched and tied. I have driven, loaded and unloaded. I have written, designed and budgeted. If it pertains to rescuing donkeys, I have not only done it; I have done it well.

I know what it means to work in 110 degrees with no shade and I have felt the bone chilling winds of a 10 degree winter. But you see I didn't do it for a boss, I did it for the donkeys. And let me tell you, if you are not doing this job for the donkeys you are in the wrong line of work.

Of all of the company owners and bosses that I know, I am the most generous. Seldom will an employee have to ask for a raise, and the ones that do seldom deserve it. I notice the extra effort, the team spirit and I reward that with financial compensation. One of J.B.'s often turned phrases when he gave me a raise was, "can't eat a pat on the back."

Every employee that has sat in my office and complained about the lack of praise has heard this dissertation. They all leave with their hat in hand and a sad look on their face. Do they really think that I am going to change? I like the way that PVDR has succeeded and a great deal of that success is due to the way Amy and I are. The way we think, the way we work and the way we handle the many stressful situations that present themselves.

**I give the donkeys my very best, every day.
Why would I expect less from you?**

WHAT IS A BRAND?

Branding and branding irons have been around since the ancient Egyptians used unique brands to identify herd animals. The practice continued with the Romans who expanded the use to include slaves. The practice has continued down through the advancement of civilization until it was imported into the Americas.

Prior to the invention of barbed wire, cattle would graze freely often mixing with the cattle of other ranchers. Brands were recorded with the local jurisdictions and would be used to settle any disputes over legitimate ownership. Horses and even donkeys were commonly branded. To be caught with a branded animal without a bill of sale from the brand owner often lead to death, whether through legal execution or not so legal lynching.

Common brands included the use of letters, symbols and lines such as:

Today, microchips are often used in lieu of a

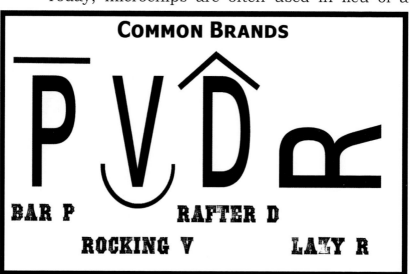

COMMON BRANDS

BAR P   RAFTER D

ROCKING V   LAZY R

physical brand.   Peaceful Valley has inserted well over three thousand microchips in donkeys that have passed though our system. This allows for permanent identification without causing undo stress or pain. The Bureau of Land Management uses a freeze brand instead of a hot brand. By soaking the brand in liquid nitrogen, the super cooled brand kills the pigment forming cell of the hair, causing it to forever grow back white. Most freeze brands are hard to read and therefore are more suitable for simple "ranch" brand and not for personal identification.

Today a brand is more likely to mean a logo or an identifiable symbol that represents a company. Coke

has a "red" that all of its bottling companies must adhere to. McDonalds Golden Arches are all made to exacting standards. Even PVDR's brand has strict characteristics:

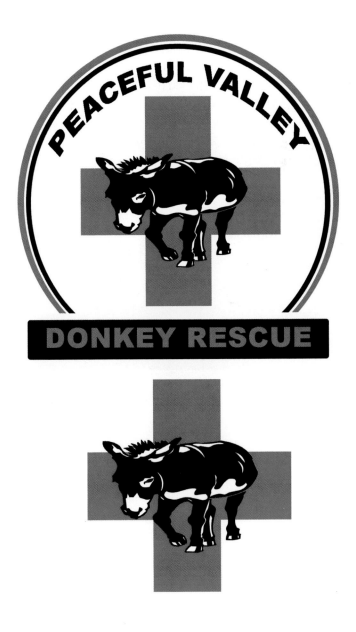

BRAND LOYALTY

Riding for the brand is an old time cowboy phrase. It means that you have pledged not only your services, but also your loyalty to the cattle company that you are working for. The Brand became your badge of honor and you not only worked hard for it, you defended it.

Today we hear "brand" and "branding" all too often. We, as a society, have been carefully molded into mindless consumers that drag ourselves through our tedious life in hopes of obtaining the newest (insert plastic Chinese made item here) with our favorite company's brand glued to the outside. Our Internet accounts are picked through to find the "keywords" that identify who we are so that the companies can better target us with their brands.

I would like to say that I am not a mindless consumer but the reality is: Branding works.

I have driven a Ford since 1986. Even when Ford sold me two of the worst designed trucks ever created, I still could not bring myself to change brands. I really cannot say if my loyalty is a result of an undying love for Ford or if I was simply too proud and couldn't allow my friends the pleasure of saying "I told you so."

Branding and logos are really one in the same. Apple Computer's apple with a bite missing, McDonalds' golden arches, Facebook's lower case f on a blue square have become more important than the products that they represent. When I was younger, Ford's blue oval was about three inches wide on the bottom left side of the tailgate, today's Fords have a blue oval that is as large as a dinner plate. These companies are using their brands to seduce you, to entice you and hopefully to sell to you. There is nothing wrong with this, it is who we are as a society.

Brand loyalty precedes even the cowboys of old. During the Dark and Middle Ages, men swore loyalty to a Lord or a King who was represented by a banner depicting a lion, bear, dragon or anything that would set this person aside from his peers. Religion has long used brand recognition: the Christian cross, the Jewish Star of David, the Wiccan five pointed star all have a clear identity all to themselves. All of these brands have been used to inspire, to intimidate and sometimes even to separate.

Symbols, logos or brands all carry power whether we choose to recognize it or not. It is what we do with that power that is important, not the image itself.

When you ride for a brand, you represent all that that brand stands for. The good, the bad and even the ugly.

The orange cruciform (C=0 M=75 Y=100 K=0) with a black donkey (C=40 Y=0 M=0 K=100) is PVDR's Brand. I would like to think it represents compassion, sacrifice and professionalism. It has been my goal that by placing my Brand on a project, on a rescue case or on any form of literature that it adds instant credibility. With the requests I get from so many rescues to add our organization's endorsement, I think it has worked.

This public image that we earned has not come easy. So many people who lack the ability to create feel compelled to try and tear down the work of others. False accusations, misleading statements and outright lies are more common than you might think in the world of animal rescue. Like with all unnecessary drama, most is inspired by jealousy. With the explosion of social media, everyone (no matter how ignorant) now has a voice and they really like to hear (or see) the force of it.

Any cause worth believing in is worth defending. People are often dumbfounded by the ferocity of my response to any insult levied against PVDR. This is not to say that I cannot take constructive criticism, but most of what I hear are outright lies. People see a guy who has sacrificed everything in an attempt to rescue donkeys and they assume that my compassion extends to people as well. An image is hard to build but easy to destroy, I never allow anyone to even attempt the later.

I live by three simple rules:

You never call my wife a bitch,
You never kick my dogs,
and you never, ever speak ill of PVDR.

LEARNIG
FROM OUR
MISTAKES

Insanity: doing the same thing over and over again and expecting different results.

A. Einstein

So many people consider the donkey to be the most stubborn of all of the creatures on earth, I beg to disagree. Man is the most stubborn and most are too dumb to realize it.

My work with the rescue takes me all over the country and I get to meet some really interesting people. Often times, these people want to impress me with their donkey skills. I'll watch them try and try and try again to accomplish something, the donkey mocking their efforts each time. I see the frustration build and they try and try and try again. More frustration, more trying...you get the picture.

Donkeys have the uncanny ability to bring out the worst in people. They will only do what they want to do and any attempt to force them otherwise will inevitably end in tears and frustration. Most abuse stems from the donkey making the handler look stupid.

I often get the privilege of being the bemused spectator. I will watch as donkeys are driven round and round in hopes of getting them to go through a particular gate or into a certain pen. Round and round, always with the donkeys ducking through the same gap. And waiting until the frustration level is almost ready to burst I'll suggest, "Go the other direction." Yep, seems simple but you would be surprised how often people will stick to a plan of action, even when it doesn't work.

I used to enjoy bass fishing. I say "used to" because I don't get much time for hobbies anymore. The thing about bass fishing is that you have to consider many factors if you are going to be a successful bass catcher and not simply a bass fisher. The time of day, the current water temperature, the clarity of the water, the under water structures, the time of year are just a handful of the things that one must take into account. After careful consideration of your data, you reach into your over stuffed tackle box and select what you hope is the perfect lure. You tie your carefully selected lure onto your line and you make your first cast. No luck, you cast again, and again, and again and maybe one more time.

But, if after five casts you have not at least had a bite, it's time to change lures. Sticking to a lure that is not working is just plain silly...so is trying to catch a donkey with a failing plan.

When the BürroCøllies and I are working a group of donkeys, we always start with Plan A. Gather the donkeys into a tight group and then push them the way we want them to go. In most cases, we can get at least half of them in the first try. We then go back and take a smaller group the same way and we keep repeating this as long as we have success each time. Once the donkeys are purposely missing the gate and running the same pattern, we stop. We take a break and let everybody settle down. Cooler heads will prevail.

Next comes Plan B. Sometimes Plan B can be as simple as moving the remaining donkeys through a different gate or even pushing the donkeys in the opposite direction that we really want them to go. Whatever the case, there is always a Plan B.

For every great idea that I have come up with that has advanced the PVDR Mission, I have had two really bad ones. I never worry about the ones that didn't work out, I just come up with something else. Without risk there can never be reward and without failure there can never really be success.

SOCIALISM & THE ART OF CATCHING DONKEYS

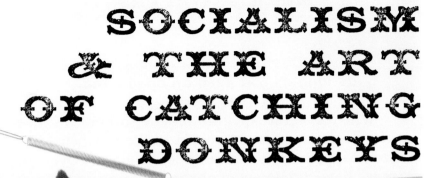

Life is full of lessons,
as long as you keep an open mind.

When we first got into donkey rescue, we were not the most experienced people in the business. We realized early on that we had a lot to learn. Over the years we have developed methods and procedures that have allowed us to do more with less physical strain and danger to the donkeys and the people.

One of my earliest lessons was in catching wild burros. There are a dozen ways to catch wild burros, most of it depends on how much time you have to dedicate to the project. Usually we are in a press for time, so the easiest plan is to set up a "wing" a long line of fencing that leads to a trap. The BürroCøllies are given instructions and away we go. The problem with this method is that wild burros are not accustomed to having dogs chase them and will usually stand and offer to fight. But like I said, if we are pinched for time this is still Plan A.

When time is not an issue, I take the lead from the government and do it real slow and sneaky.

Wild Burros, like people, live under the illusion that they are free and can do as they please. Push them too hard or too fast and they will inevitably push back. So instead of pushing, I give them a little incentive while taking away a little freedom. I find a spot where the burros are comfortable and dump out a couple bags of feed and set up one side of the trap. The burros will be a little wary of the new obstruction but the feed more than makes up for it. I go out everyday, at the same time, and dump more feed.

After a week, I dump extra feed and set up another side of the trap. Everyday I head out and dump the new larger amount of feed, always at the same time. By this time it is obvious that burros are waiting on me to bring their feed. It is also obvious that they are staying close to the trap and not wandering too far so they don't miss out.

The third week brings another side to the trap and yet even more feed. Now we begin to see new burros standing around the trap trying to get in on a good thing. You might even notice a few of the jacks fighting with one another but that is to be expected. You see, they no longer have to forage far and wide to find enough grazing so they get bored and need to blow off a little stream. Same system, same time...extra feed.

By the fourth week I set up the last side of the trap with gate in it. Dump in the feed, jump in the truck, drive a bit down the road and walk back to the trap. I then close the gate and complete the project. By the time I am finished, the burros had already freely given up their freedom for a handout.

And that, my friends, is why so many Americans look to the government for support. I guess the trick works on a lot more than just wild burros.

As a history buff, I am always surprised at the loss of freedom that the American people have endured over the past 150 years. Every aspect of our lives are controlled by a law, an agency or a tax. I guess the trade off to this is all the freebies that most Americans have come to expect and rely on. Personally, I don't want ANYTHING from the government, nor will I allow PVDR to accept anything from them. So many non-profits accept government hand outs, and so many have had to change their mission to appease the politicians and agenda that is now funding it.

W.T.S.D.

When Things Settle Down is an often turned phrase around PVDR.

You might hear, "When things settle down, I want to paint the outside of the medical building."

Or, "When things settle down, we should build a training arena."

Or even, "When things settle down, we need to replace the roof on the hay barn."

Thing is...things never settle down.

Every year since its incorporation in 2000, PVDR has grown in size, donkeys, scope, geographic region and assets...every single year. No matter how many we rescue, there is always a never ending stream of requests for more.

My greatest fear is what is going to happen when we are worn out? Who is going to pick up the reins and keep this organization on course? I would look to my sons but they have their own plans, their own lives and it would not be fair to guilt them into taking on something that is this all-consuming if their hearts weren't in it.

We have gotten better over the years. Instead of me killing myself with every project, we have developed systems, methods and equipment to make the job not only physically easier but a lot safer too. Specially designed chutes and alleyways, a custom built hydraulic tilt squeeze are just a few of the improvements that make PVDR more efficient. But this organization requires a lot more than just physical labor.

It demands a level of commitment that most people just don't have anymore. It is not uncommon for those of us on the transport teams to be away from home for days or weeks, traveling thousands of miles and missing our families. It requires intelligence to juggle all of the many responsibilities. It requires charisma to win the public over to the donkey's side. And finally it requires strength. Not only physical strength but strength of character. The strength to defend the organization, the strength to face any crisis, the strength to put your self aside and make decisions that are in the best interest of PVDR.

So far, I have always had that level of strength and dedication. So far...

In July of 2009 I was diagnosed with bladder cancer. After 5 surgeries and an ongoing chemo regiment, I am doing well. Battling cancer has been an inconvenience but I never once allowed it to interfere with my duties at the rescue. I would like to take this opportunity to thank Dr. Cook for his expertise as well as his calm approach. Amy and I have no doubt that had I remained under treatment in California, I would not have an intact bladder today.

But for some reason, this past year has been tough on me. The ever present aches and pains are becoming harder to ignore and I have had to admit to myself that I might not be the strongest, toughest most invincible person on the planet anymore. This year I can honestly say that I am feeling my age. Less than 50 might not seem too old, but I have worked in construction since I was 18 years old and I have spent the last 12 years of my life pushing 650 pound donkeys around. I am just getting worn out.

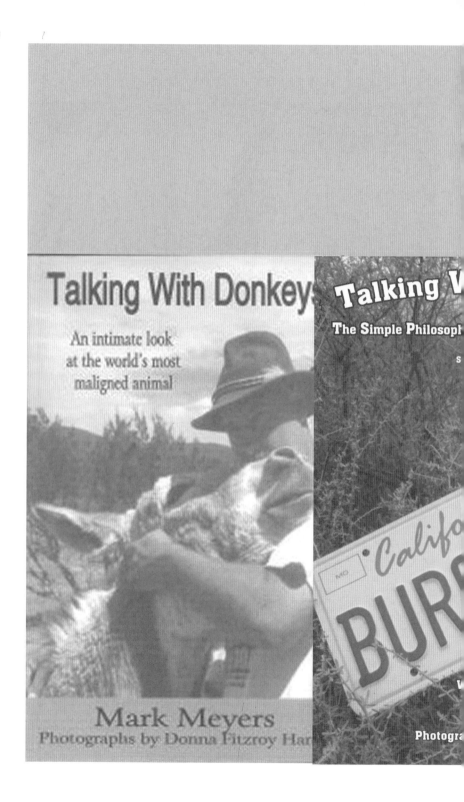

Talking With Donkey

An intimate look
at the world's most
maligned animal

Mark Meyers
Photographs by Donna Fitzroy Har

Talking W

The Simple Philosoph

Califo

BUR

Photogr

h Donkey

21st Century Burro

dition

on by **Mark S. Me**
with **Jesse M**

oy **Donna FitzRoy**
and **Frank J. S**

ia

MAN

Talking With
Donkeys
Third Edition

saving them all

Written & Photographed by Mark S. Meyers

Talking With Donkeys

An intimate look
at the world's most
maligned animal

Mark Meyers
Photographs by Donna Fitzroy Hardy

I began work on the first Talking With Donkeys in the Fall of 2004. I liked the idea of a book about donkeys for donkey owners. I had absolutely no idea what I was doing and I couldn't find anybody that was interested in helping, so I just did.

I had written several articles that had been published in various newspapers, magazines and websites so I started with those. I then added several of the fund raising stories that I had along with stories from my many pack trips across Death Valley. And for filler, I included topics that I had spoken about at various service clubs around the country.

A dear friend of mine was kind enough to take the pictures for the book and I added a few of my own. Another friend designed the cover. I didn't know what was the difference between CYMK and RGB. I also had no clue what a "bleed" was or any of the other technical jargon that the printing house kept throwing at me.

I had one thousand copies of the book printed and I cannot tell you the pride you feel when you open that first box and pick up the first copy. I feel bad for today's authors who publish everything online and will never experience that rush.

TWD1 is chock full of typos and misspelled words. It is also considered by many to be my finest work. It is a sincere piece of my soul, something that I would usually never bare. TWD1 completely sold out in the first six months after I had it printed. I have found used copies online for over $100.00 with signed copies going even higher.

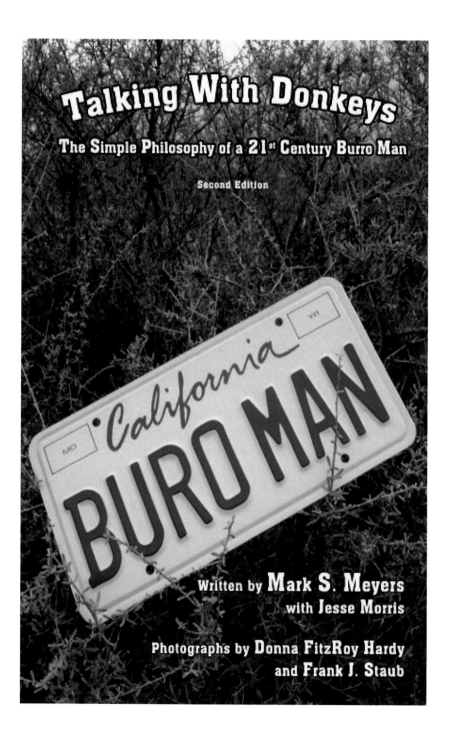

TWD2 is my least favorite of the series. I liked the original concept of writing stories that revolved around my personal philosophies but the end result just wasn't me. Thinking that the book would be better with a real writer on board, I used a co-writer on the project. The end result was a bunch of crap that totally missed my point and sounded nothing like me. In one story he actually stuck in the word "tummy".

This time around we were a little more savvy about how to set up the book for publishing, but still had a lot to learn. Many of the aspects of the book are too small to see comfortably and the picture quality is lacking in many shots.

We did manage to sell almost 2,500 copies and only have a few remaining in our gift shop. People who liked it best were the ones that did not know me personally or had not read the previous book. I am probably being too hard on it as we did receive a large amount of praise for the book.

I am eventually going to re-print this version and put it back into my words. I think the core messages are spot on and are worth telling.

Talking With
Donkeys
Third Edition

saving them all

Written & Photographed by Mark S. Meyers

When it was written, TWD3 was the exact book that I wanted to write. I did everything myself for this book. I wrote it, took the pictures and did all of the layout myself using a very sophisticated publishing program. I did try to keep costs down by limiting the page count and the end result is a book crammed full of stuff.

Most of TWD3 was written while I was living alone in Texas. I was charged with building PVDR's presence in West Texas and had to endure long absences from my family. I used the time to write.

TWD3 explains the problems faced by donkeys in the United States and PVDR's solution to those problems. It outlines how we went from a small backyard hobby into being the largest organization in the country. It also lays out exactly how PVDR intends to Save Them All. It contains some light hearted stories from our life on the ranch and my adventures catching donkeys around the country.

An interesting side note to TWD3 is that 30 copies were purchased by a professor of literature at a Florida college. He used the book as a platform to encourage his writing students to create their own style. It is funny in a way on account of me being so uneducated but still managed to make it to college!

THE WORLD FAMOUS BURRO COLLIES

Rescuing donkeys made me realize something about myself; a 6'4" 245 pound man cannot run fast. It has also taught me that a 48" 500 pound donkey can run fast. Whatever is a donkey rescuer to do?

A man who shot donkeys as part of his job suggested that I use dogs. Yes, he was a man who shot donkeys as part of his job...but that did not mean that he couldn't make a valid suggestion.

I began my pursuit by looking into all of the working breeds. Some breeds are designed to push and some to gather. There are some who use aggression and others that use finesse. There are those that are smart and can think on their own and others that rely on pure instinct.

I took some time and looked into livestock to see how cattle, sheep and goats reacted to dogs in general. Donkeys are extremely aggressive towards dogs so my dogs would have to be tough as nails but also smart enough to over ride their instincts when placed in a dangerous situation. Donkeys are fast, capable of speeds over 30 miles per hour. Donkeys seldom run from danger but when they do, they do at some amazing speeds. My dogs would have to match and exceed the speed of the donkeys if they were to be of any real use.

The biggest difference in catching or moving donkeys versus other types of livestock is that they tend to push back. Even wild burros will only move off far enough to feel safe, but they seldom turn tail and run away. They feel much safer keeping a wary eye on anything that threatens them. Cattle, sheep and even horses can be pushed in a direction; donkeys are much more difficult to drive.

With my list of requirements, I went dog shopping. I looked at all of the old breeds and many of the new ones. People have been perfecting the "stock dog" in this country for over a hundred years. I even considered buying an older dog that had already been trained to run stock. I realized that it took me many years of practical experience to be able to read a situation and learn what the donkeys were going to do. If I bought a trained dog the chances of it being able to adapt to a new set of rules were slim. I needed my own dog to train.

I found Bønney in Tehachapi, CA. She was seven weeks old and was half border collie and half Australian Shepherd. I like the Border Collies as they want to please. They can be fast, they are extremely intelligent and they can work both ends of the donkey. The Australian Shepherd brings not only additional herding instinct but also adds size. In working donkeys, size matters.

Bønney became my constant companion both on the ranch and at home. She learned to move donkeys by watching and assisting me. I was living alone in Texas at the time and had around fifty donkeys at our first little facility in Miles, TX. I had set up feed alleys that I would rotate the donkeys through every few hours. It was the perfect way to teach Bønney how to push and how to communicate with me. For those many months, Bønney and I figured out what it meant to be a burro collie.

The hardest part of working with any animal is communication. Conveying what needed to be done with commands both verbal and with my hands. Bønney and I began the communication system that we still use today:

Come By: Move in from the left and drive the donkeys clockwise.
Away: Move in from the right and move the donkeys counterclockwise.
Out: Leave the pen, move outside of the fence.
Down: Drop to the ground.
Come: Run to me
That'll Do: Break off, the job is done.
Leave It: Do not touch or push. Can be a donkey or even a piece of food.
Crate: Time for bed.
Whet-Che-Che: Starting moving the donkeys.
Put Em Up: Push the donkeys into the trap or pen.

Later on, we added names so that each dog would know that the command was for them "Bønney Come By" and then we added "Dogs" as in "Dogs Come" so that they knew all of them were being addressed. But I am getting ahead of myself.

Bønney grew into the smartest most loyal dog that I could have ever asked for. Once she learned how the donkeys reacted, she exploited her knowledge and was able to move the donkeys with almost no effort. She "had the touch" and could almost read the donkey's minds. The dog thing was really working, but I came to realize that one dog could handle 10 donkeys but what about 100? So...we found Bütchie.

Bütchie belonged to my idiot redneck neighbor. His only experience with people, except for the few times he was able to sneak over to my house, was to be picked up and thrown into a dark shed. The reason for the shed was due to the fact that the city kept complaining about Bütchie getting loose. After being given another warning, the neighbor came out side and asked if I wanted him, Bønney and I had another teammate.

My neighbor might have been an idiot but he knew dogs. Bütchie was a natural. He was only three months when he came on board but he fell right in. He was timid around people and would pee all over himself if I raised my voice, but we built a bond. Bütchie was my "ton of bricks" and his toughness was obvious. I now had the intelligence in Bønney and the strength in Butchie. The only thing we were lacking was speed. So, enter BigTimë.

I purchased BigTimë through a breeder in North Texas much to the distaste of many. I was attacked on the Internet for buying from a breeder instead of getting a dog from a rescue. "Oh so you rescue donkeys but you buy dogs?" In our lifetime, Amy and I have rescued dozens of dogs. All of them were great pets but we took them for what they were and accepted the baggage that came with them.

In my search for working dogs, I needed tools. When I was a contractor, I did not shop at the dollar store for the tools of my trade. I did not try to make a hammer out of a screwdriver. I always used the right tool for the right job. How many rescue dogs would I have to go through to find one that was right for the job? And what to do with the ones that didn't work out? And what about the ones who would be killed because their instincts were not right and their reactions too slow?

BigTimë is a full blood Border Collie. He is smaller than Bønney and Bütchie but with a work ethic that puts them both to shame. BigTimë is always on, he is what trainers term as an "intense dog". The first thing we had to do was curb BigTimë's instinct to run out ahead of the donkeys and stop them. His instinct was to gather and not let them run away. The instinct was so strong that it was impossible to break him of it. So instead I let him run out ahead and then continue to the rear of the herd. You can imagine how fast dog a must be to run ahead of the donkeys and then back to the drags. BigTimë is far and away the fastest dog I have ever seen.

And finally, BlüeBønnet. One of the difficulties in our line of work is the heat and the ever present hazard of heat exhaustion. Dogs, especially black dogs are very susceptible to heat exhaustion. Because of the need to rotate the dogs in and out of the truck to allow them to cool off, I was often left shorthanded. Adding another dog gives me the flexibility of working them in pairs and different combinations.

BlüeBønnet is a registered Australian Shepherd. I purchased her from a breeder near Lubbock, TX. These particular dogs were worked on cattle and I was able to meet the parents and grandparents of the puppy I chose. Australian Shepherds are bigger boned than Border Collies and lack the speed. They are a strong dog with the ability to work both ends of an animal.

Photo by Craig Edwards candysaussies.com

So this is how it works. We set up on the donkeys, this could be in one of the ranch paddocks or out in the wilds of some desert. We have a direction and a destination. I give the commands and the dogs run off. The dogs run to the backside of the donkeys and get them gathered and moving. Bütchie has the hardest job as he has to run along all of the donkeys and get them moving. Bønney helps but works on the strays, quietly pushing them towards the destination. BigTimë runs the entire group, shaping them into a line. Bütchie and BlüeBønnet keeps pushing, Bonney keeps an eye out for stragglers and BigTimë keeps running up and down the line. It is absolute poetry.

Every few minutes each dog will break off and look at me. They are waiting for another command to ensure that they are doing the right thing. Many stock dog trainers do not like this in a dog. They feel that it shows a lack of confidence. Maybe if we worked the same pens every day, with the same animals, I could agree with this line of thought. But we don't. Every situation that we find ourselves in is unique. If the dogs make a wrong decision it could mean losing the donkeys and pushing them far away from our traps.

These dogs have become a vital part of the donkey rescue. Their ability to get the job done is both irreplaceable and humbling. They are my constant companions and have collectively logged over a million miles in the truck. They travel from coast to coast, border to border not knowing what their next job will be, but always ready to work.

www.burrocollies.com
www.facebook.com/burrocollies
www.twitter.com/burrocollies

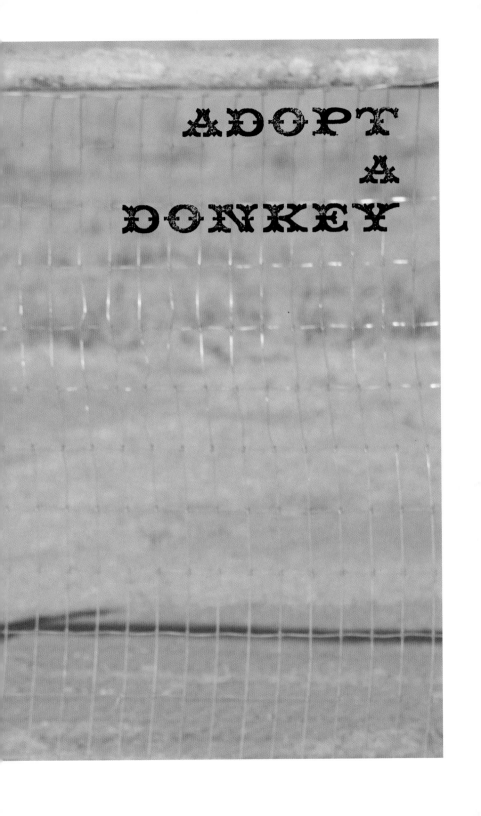

ADOPT
A
DONKEY

Peaceful Valley has a lot of donkeys. We rescue ever increasing numbers each year. With so many donkeys coming into the system we must move others out to make room. The easiest way is to find loving adoptive homes.

Typically, a perspective PVDR adopter is a person on a smaller sized ranch who is looking for a couple of pets. While some donkeys make excellent guardians, we do not adopt them out for this purpose. Some donkeys have been known to kill smaller animals and the complications that would be created if one of our adopted donkeys killed someone's animals are simply not worth it for us.

The donkeys that are available through our adoption program are friendly towards people, will accept a halter and will allow their hooves to be trimmed. As the largest rescue in the land, we do not have the time or manpower to train them any further than that. Many of the donkeys are more than capable of being trained and many have been trained to ride, drive and pack by their adoptive families.

One issue that has scared off some of our adopters is the clause in our adoption agreement that states that the donkeys will always belong to PVDR. This is done for a couple of reasons. One, we don't want the donkey sold into a bad situation, we don't want the donkeys to be unnecessarily euthanized for an ailment that we may be able to treat and we want to be able to take the donkey back should things go wrong.

In one case, the donkeys were involved in a divorce dispute. The people didn't have kids to fight over so they fought over the donkeys. They both claimed they wanted them but neither was feeding them. We were able to present our signed agreement and collect

Adopt a donkey... adopt a friend

Contact your local Satellite Adoption Center
or visit www.donkeyrescue.org

our donkeys without being tied up in a legal battle. The requirements for adoption are pretty simple. We expect the donkeys to have shelter appropriate to the climate they will be living in. This varies by region as what is adequate in Southern California will not be appropriate in Upstate New York. We want the adopters to provide quality feed and medical care as required. We want the adoptive family to spend time with the donkeys and not just leave them to their own devices.

A few things that do not work for us is boarding facilities. Many adopters want to adopt a donkey and then put it in a stall somewhere else. These donkeys are used to companionship both from donkeys and people, tucking them away in a boarding facility just doesn't make sense. Another issue we have is Christmas presents. So many people want to get a donkey for a parent as a present. The problem with this is that we can't do a home inspection, we won't have a signed agreement from the person actually receiving the donkey and the person won't have the opportunity to pick out their own donkey. We suggest that they give the person a certificate for adoption that they can redeem on their own after the holidays.

PROJECT SANCTUARY

An operation on the scale of PVDR is an expensive undertaking. Our biggest expense is feeding the many donkeys that are under our care. Aside from the ever fluctuating cost of hay, there is the expense of labor to distribute it, equipment to move it and facilities to store it.

In 2010, we piloted a project where we placed 100 formerly wild burros on 1,000 acres of pasture. We monitored what they ate, where they roamed and how they dealt with rain and other weather issues. After 6 months, we collected the burros and gave them a thorough evaluation. All of them had healthier looking coats, their hooves were in excellent shape and they were all in good body condition. We released them again and found that after another six months, all we're still in great health. This particular group of burros were older (15+ year or older) that had come from the BLM Sale Program. They were not aggressive but definitely did not want to be friendly towards humans. Living on this large sanctuary was a way for us to give them back a modicum of freedom. It also saved us over $30,000 on their feed.

On average, it costs PVDR $42.00 per month to feed a donkey on one of our ranches. Donkeys living on a sanctuary cost us only $15.00 per month.

Based on this initial test, we launched Project Sanctuary in full force. At first our luck held out and we successfully put several hundred donkeys onto grazing leases in Texas and Oklahoma. The donkeys were healthy and we were able to control our feed costs. Then in 2011 the Texas Drought wreaked havoc on our plans. The grazing was all used up and with no rain, there would not be anymore. We had to bring many of the donkeys back onto our ranch.

The drought had a terrible impact on all of Texas agriculture. Many farmers went bust and millions of cattle were sold off for pennies on the dollar. In the long run PVDR benefitted from this sell off. Once the rains returned in 2012, many ranches were without their cattle and the owners were more than happy to lease us their land.

Project Sanctuary was a rough sell to our donor base. They were concerned that the donkeys were being turned out to fend for themselves never to be seen again. Some even accused us of abandoning our responsibilities. With a little discussion, we were able to convince everyone (well most everyone) that this was a solid plan.

The donkeys have a local person who keeps a constant check on the fencing, water supply and the availability of quality forage. The donkeys are usually alternated between pastures that are roughly 500 acres in size. This allows for a PVDR staff member to look at all of the donkeys on a regular basis. If any are in any type of distress they can be easily removed and taken back to our ranch. The donkeys living on sanctuary are typically gathered twice per year for a complete medical inspection.

Our wild burro population gets first dibs on sanctuary openings. They have the least chance of being adopted and prefer the open spaces to living on the ranch. Sanctuary donkeys are in no way given a life sentence, many have been returned to our ranch because they have become too friendly and will do better on our adoption program.

TILT
CHUTE

PVDR has always been on the cutting edge, not only in donkey rescue but also in donkey maintenance. Handling so many donkeys we have had to come up with many solutions to problems. One huge problem is the fact that we deal with so many wild burros that have to be trimmed but imply refuse to allow it. These burros, some in excess of 700 pounds, can be dangerous. In 2009, I worked with a company in Oklahoma to design a chute that would not only squeeze, but tilt as well. This company specializes in these machines designed for cattle. A donkey's physiology is much different than a cow's so we have to redesign many aspects. I also insisted that it be made portable as it is much easier to move the equipment than to move the burros.

We have successfully used this machine hundreds of times. It not only saves on time but it is much easier on the burros than sedation. Even with sedation, many of the burros can still be dangerous and would have to be put completely under and laid on the ground. With this machine, two people can trim a donkey in less than 15 minutes start to finish.

The tilt operates on an electrically driven hydraulic system. There are separate controls for the front door, rear door, body squeeze and two leg squeezes. Once the donkey walks in, we squeeze him down so that he cannot move. His legs are secured with ropes and the chute is tilted on its side. The bottom drops out and allows the hooves to be trimmed. Once the bottom is closed, the chute is lowered and the donkey can walk out.

MAJOR PROJECTS

US Fish & Wildlife Service
Sheldon Refuge, NV

In 2003, we were asked to get involved with the capture and removal of wild burros on the Sheldon Refuge located in the extreme North-West corner of Nevada. This refuge is managed by the US Fish and Wildlife Service and they were having an issue with the wild horses and burros destroying the native habitat.

PVDR has always been an animal rescue, we are not an animal activist group. There is an extreme difference between the two. Activists file lawsuits, they challenge policies, they picket and they hire lobbyists. Animal rescues just rescue animals.

I am often attacked because of our work with the Federal Government. Many activists do not want the burros and horses removed. They claim, and by most accounts I agree, that the government is systematically decimating the wild horse and burros herds. These activists often challenge us over our projects and insist that we join them in their cause. But again, PVDR is an animal rescue.

If we didn't work with the government, who would be there for the burros? I do not have to like the policies to help ensure the safety of these burros. Wild burros, especially jacks, are hard to place with the general public, so if we didn't take them who would?

So back to my story...

We helped establish a safe capture program and began removing the burros. Here are the statistics on this ongoing project.

2003-41   **2004-16**
2005-15   **2009-109**
2012-92

In the Fall 2012, Zac and I performed the latest phase. We transported 92 burros over 7,500 miles in 11 days. We began by driving from Texas to our Satellite in Scenic Arizona. We offloaded corral panels and set up a temporary holding facility complete with hay and water.

We drove to the Sheldon Refuge and loaded up both trailers and brought Group A back to Scenic. Then we returned to the Sheldon for the rest. These were also taken to Scenic and offloaded. Group A was then reloaded and driven to Texas. PVDR has strict guidelines for the safe transportation of our donkeys. The distance from the Sheldon to our Texas Facility was too great to do in one stretch. By allowing the burros a respite in Scenic, they all arrived in Texas in good health.

There was one tragedy while performing this rescue. An elderly jennet with a few day old foal at her side died while at the Scenic holding facility. She was in poor health and the fact that she foaled so late in the year meant that she has other issues as well. Her foal was bottle fed and cared for by our wonderful volunteers. The foal was named Sheldon 2.0 after the original Sheldon. The original Sheldon was from our very first capture and he went on to be adopted into a wonderful home in Texas. Despite the veterinarians efforts the original Sheldon died just prior to the start of this phase.

We see.
We hear.
We feel.
We matter.

Please support the Peaceful
Valley Donkey Rescue and
their campaign to
improve the plight of the
American Donkey.

www.donkeyrescue.org

The original Sheldon

Bureau of Land Management
Various States

In 2004, Congress passed a law stating that all wild horses and burros that were captured by the BLM, over the age of 10, had to be sold rather than granted the protection of the Federal Wild Horse and Burro Act. This new law also affected any wild horse or burro that had been offered for adoption three times without success.

These older burros are the hardest to adopt into loving homes as many of them are battle scarred, missing ears and partially blind. Having been captured later in life, they are sometimes more difficult to gentle and some can be outright dangerous.

Under the law, these burros must be sold and can not be given away. So in order to fulfill the law PVDR pays a token amount per burro rescued. We take as many as we can to ensure that these older burros will have a safe haven to live out their lives. Castrating older donkeys can have complications, so any of these sale burros that do not show signs of aggression are left intact and kept separated from any females.

All of the sale burros are easily recognizable because of the addition of a second larger US brand. This brand signifies that the burro is no longer protected by the federal government. Whenever possible, these burros are placed on sanctuary so that they can live out their lives with a sense of freedom.

Project Statistics:

2005-14	2006-120
2007-91	2009-9
2010-13	2011-49
2012-11	

Humane Society of the United States
Kona, HI

In 2011, working in conjunction with the Humane Society of the United States, Peaceful Valley Donkey Rescue flew 120 wild burros from Kona, Hawaii to Los Angeles California.

Donkeys have existed on the Hawaiian Islands since the days of colonization. They were used in the sugar cane and coffee fields and were also a useful form of transportation. It is unknown where these donkeys originated but they have thrived in this tropical paradise.

At the conclusion of World War II, there was a surplus of army jeeps on the islands. These were extremely cheap and were bought up by local farmers and used to replace the donkeys in their various functions. Left with no use, the donkeys moved off into the interior of the islands and established themselves into herds.

On the Hawaiian Big Island of Kona, a continuing drought wreaked havoc on the islands grass and other vegetation. The donkeys were forced out of their areas and onto golf courses and other places where that could find food and water. The donkeys were considered a safety risk as many were getting struck on the busy roads.

A local veterinarian, Dr. Brady Bergin, took up the cause and put together a plan to gather and remove the burros. Many burros were placed locally with the help of many dedicated volunteers. Dr Bergin castrated all captured males. But even with Dr Bergin and his associates work, there was still a surplus of burros.

The HSUS got involved and came up with the idea to fly the donkeys off of the island, the problem they faced was to where?

PVDR is the largest rescue in the United States, there are few organizations that can step up and take in 120 equine and have the resources to pull it off. Aside from the sheer number of animals, there were many other logistical problems that had to be addressed. Transportation from the airport, quarantine facilities at the ranch, additional feed and labor, just to name a few.

In early September 2011, Amy and I flew to Kona Hawaii to begin PVDR's phase of the project. With the help of volunteers, we loaded the 119 burros into trailers and drove them to the airport. The burros then had to be transferred into the stock crates. These crates were sitting on the airport luggage dollies and were pulled up behind each trailer in turn. I would then push six donkeys into each crate. The crates were driven to a specially designed 747, loaded using a scissor lift and then locked into place.

The flight home was uneventful and the donkeys all remained calm. Landing at LAX, the donkeys were transferred from the plane to the dollies and then picked up with a forklift and lifted to the back of the waiting trailers. I again had to go into each crate and push the donkeys out.

All in all the project was a huge success. We did have an issue with some of the geldings. After a few deaths, we realized that their immune systems were compromised. Living and breeding on an island had left them susceptible to everything. With a great deal of effort on the part of PVDR staff, we were able to reverse the condition of the worst effected and save the majority. These Hawaiian Burros are now living in Texas.

In hind-sight if I had it to do over again, I would not have moved the burros that close to winter. I would have performed the rescue in the Spring, allowing them more time to adjust. I also would not have had them castrated prior to stress of the flight. These things were not in PVDR's control but we will remember the lesson.

Louisiana Neglect Case
DeRidder, LA

The caller ID showed that is was a Louisiana phone number and I almost didn't answer. We have been busier than ever these past few months and I knew I did not have time to help him. Texas is still abandoning donkeys at record rates, we are moving hundreds of donkeys around on new grazing leases AND I am closing our California facility and moving all of those donkeys (and other critters) to Texas. I did not have the time for Louisiana troubles on top of everything else...

I knew what the deputy wanted. A rescue case had just come across from the Internet from him. A cruelty case involving 65+ donkeys. I knew it involved an elderly man who kept breeding them even when there was no market for them. I also knew that he couldn't afford to feed them and they were literally starving.

"There is only so much we can do." "There are only so many hours in a week" are a few of things that went through my already exhausted mind...but I picked up the phone anyway.

Zac and I arrived in Beauregard Parish, LA the next day with two trucks and our largest two trailers. I had met the deputy down the road and he had filled me in with the particulars. An 89 year old man had way too many donkeys, the donkeys were in terrible shape, the Parish and the local Humane Society didn't have the money or resources to help on a case this big. The deputy didn't want to accompany us to the man's house because he knew his presence would just upset the man.

When we stepped out of the truck I was hit with two things that I was not prepared for...there were a lot more than 65 donkeys and this old man reminded me of my dad who I lost to cancer in April.

In these types of cases, it is always good to have a bad guy. Someone to blame, somebody to take my anger out on. This dear old man had been widowed five years ago, he had no children, he was obviously not able to care for himself and he was in tears over the condition of his donkeys. So I did what you would have done in my shoes, I cried with him and told him I would take care of everything.

Oh, and the other thing I wasn't prepared for? There were 82 donkeys, not 65+.

With the exception of 11 adult jacks, all of the donkeys were Jennets with last year's baby still nursing and they were pregnant again. These poor girls were all exceptionally thin and the babies were nursing them down to skin and bones. We had to get them back to our ranch ASAP but with this many we were going to have to make two trips.

It costs PVDR around $1000 for every donkey that we rescue. This includes the actual cost of the rescue (fuel, hotels, truck maintenance, etc), the processing (microchips, worming, vaccinations), medical care, castration for the males, pregnancy care and at least one year's feed. So in this case we are looking at around $80,000, not counting the +\- 35 babies we could expect next spring.

As a side note to this story:

We released the details of this case on Facebook, which we often do. Several people took it upon themselves to call the Beauregard Parish Sheriff Department to validate our claims. The dispatcher told them she had no idea what they were talking about. These same people then accused us of fabricating the whole story.

Couple of things here. One, we would not have gotten involved if the original case wasn't instigated by a law enforcement agency. This is a standard policy for us as we are just too busy. Second, there was never an animal cruelty case opened so therefore no one except the deputy knew much about it.

Now maybe there are a lot of organizations out there that need to lie about what they do...we are not one of them. I think some people just have way too much time on their hands and would rather try and tear something down as opposed to build something up.

United States Department of Agriculture
Presidio, TX

Peaceful Valley has been working in conjunction with the US Department of Agriculture along the Mexican Border in South West Texas since 2008. Many wild burros as well as domestic donkeys move in and out of the Big Bend Ranch State Park and Mexico. When captured, these donkeys are transferred to PVDR.

Donkeys are often used to smuggle drugs and other contraband into the United States. Once the donkeys are unloaded, they are released to fend for themselves. Many of the donkeys rescued in this area carry Mexican brands and scarification. They also show signs of severe abuse and carry scars just above the hoof line where they have been hobbled with wire.

Texas Wildlife and Parks Service has temporarily stopped shooting the burros in the Big Bend State Park and are trying to find a solution for their removal. The difficulty in removing the burros is the harshness and inaccessibility of the land, restrictions on where the donkeys can be trapped and the enormous cost of the project. PVDR has agreed to take any burros removed from the Park if and when they are caught.

SOUTH WEST BORDER PROJECT

Texas County Sheriff Departments
Various locations throughout Texas

In 2011, Texas dried up and blew away. The weather people said it was a La Niña year, but all we knew is that it never rained. PVDR buys tens of thousands of tons of hay each year. No rain meant no hay and we were hard pressed to find any at all. We were forced to purchase hay from states as far away as South Dakota at high prices and usually of poor quality. In the end we were able to get enough hay to last the year but that was only half our problem.

The other half? **Texans started dumping their donkeys by the hundreds.**

Since PVDR set up shop in Texas back in 2008, we have always had to deal with donkey abandonment. Back then it was usually all jacks being dumped along some deserted stretch of highway. Jacks had no financial value and simply won't sell at auction. Instead of wasting feed on them, ranchers were abandoning them. Ranchers would allow the donkeys to freely breed in order to get Jennets. Female donkeys make better livestock guardians especially if raised around them. Jacks are wholly unsuited for the task.

We began to work with county Sheriff Departments throughout the state. The numbers were not overly ridiculous and we felt that we were handling the problem. It became evident that people were taking their donkeys several counties away from their home. Since everyone that lives rurally knows what animals belong where, the donkeys couldn't be dumped too close to home for fear they would be recognized.

In 2011 when it became evident that the drought was not going to break, people in Texas found themselves in a desperate situation. Their grazing was gone and their stock tanks were dry. Most were faced with either buying feed and hauling water or selling off their stock. Many chose to sell.

As these ranchers de-stocked their ranches, many of these ranches are thousands of acres, they realized that they had more donkeys than they thought. It was a common experience to receive a half dozen calls per week from some rancher wanting us to take 20 donkeys off of his ranch. As we were swamped with law enforcement cases, we would have to decline. This left these ranchers with no other options. No sale yard in the state would allow a donkey to be unloaded, people were running them through the sale but not picking them up when they didn't sell.

In 2011, during the height of the drought we brought in over 700 abandoned donkeys, all from Sheriff Departments. In 2012, as the rains returned, we had hoped that the worst was behind us. Unfortunately the trend continued and we brought in another 475 abandoned donkeys.

PVDR started 2013 with over 150 donkeys on open rescue cases all from Sheriff Departments. There appears to be no end in sight.

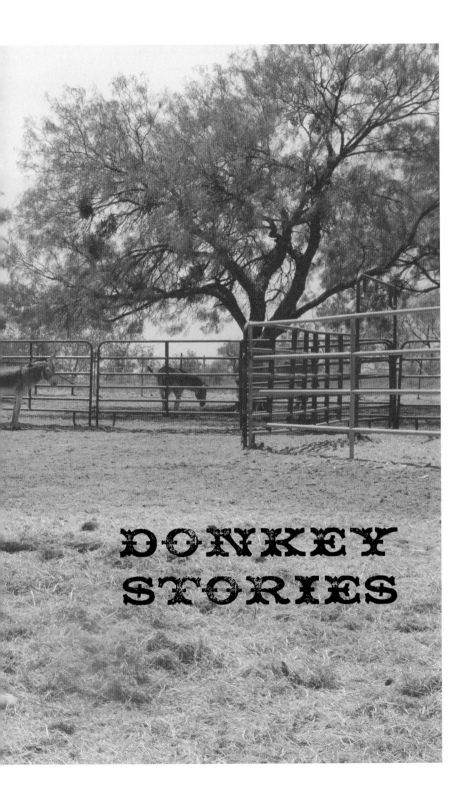

DONKEY
STORIES

The Story of Hope

Awhile back I was in North Carolina dropping off some donkeys at our Satellite Adoption Facility when a call came in from a Sheriff's Department near Waco, Texas. The deputy was responding to several complaints about some starving donkeys. His county didn't have the money or resources to hire someone to come and catch and hold the donkeys so he called us.

There were a family of 5 donkeys on a little piece of land and they had stripped everything edible. I told him that it would take me two days to get there but I was on my way. He promised to go and buy hay with his own money so that the donkeys would have something to eat in the meantime.

Since I was so worried about these donkeys, the dogs and I drove straight through the night and we got there 28 hours later. What I saw broke my heart...

There were four donkeys: a jack and three young jennets. All of them were skin and bones, they were so emaciated that they didn't even try and resist when I put a halter on them and lead them to the trailer. As there was no one around when I arrived, I called the deputy and asked about the fifth donkey that was nowhere to be seen. He said that there had been five, so I started looking around.

The property was a junk yard and I mean junk. No one lived there and it was obvious that the donkeys had been dumped off to fend for themselves. I followed a shallow creek bed and there I found the remains of the fifth donkey. She had been run down by wild hogs and killed. You know I don't like using gory pictures so I will spare you the details, but this terrible scene brought tears to my eyes. This poor jennet was pregnant, starving and completely unable to defend herself or run away.

While I was trying to compose myself, my phone rang again.

Same story as the last: 17 starving donkeys abandoned on a bare piece of land. I laid my hand on the dead jenny's head and closed my eyes. I wanted to apologize for all she had been through but the words got stuck in my throat. It was a four hour drive to the next rescue and this time I wasn't going to be too late.

This time the donkeys were not only thin, but many had really long hooves too. They had obviously been locked up in a small space to prevent them from eating the food that was probably intended for cattle. The loading went pretty smoothly until I turned to the last three donkeys that were laying down. They had trouble getting up and as I helped each one onto their feet, I noticed that they couldn't bend their legs. They could walk but in a strange stiff legged way. There were two older jennets and one of them had a little

baby.

I had the vet meet me at the ranch so that he could assess the whole group as soon as possible. What he found was pretty typical of starving donkeys and he set up a feeding program to ensure that they could safely put back on the weight they so desperately needed. The other three were a different story.

He diagnosed these three with neurological damage, probably a result of eating toxins. Donkeys will eat anything to prevent starvation. The Texas drought has forced many donkeys into eating things that they typically wouldn't. These two adult jennets had eaten something really bad and the mom had passed it through her milk to the baby. The vet had high hopes for the jennet's full recovery but he was really worried about the baby. She could not nurse from her mother anymore and if she was to have a chance, we were going to have to bottle feed her and monitor her around the clock.

I knew that I didn't have the time to care for a baby around the clock, not with all of my other responsibilities but I couldn't get the image of that poor pregnant jennet out of my mind. Maybe if I had been quicker she and her baby might not have been killed, so I gathered the staff together and detailed the plan. I explained to them how this was her only hope and I guess it stuck because we all call her Hope and we are trying everything in our power to make it come true.

It is what it is...

This is my very own personal mantra. I usually end up saying it at least once every day. What it means is that I don't need to worry about things that are out of my control. I only need to handle each situation as it presents itself.

Two recent rescues, on two consecutive days brought my mantra into use once again.

Like always, it began with a phone call. A North Texas farmer had a donkey with a "lump on his head". He told me that the donkey probably wasn't worth the trip and if we didn't want him he could just shoot him. I know you probably hear a lot of people using this threat, but in Texas it is a promise not a threat. Just last week we picked up 12 starving donkeys, the owner had already shot 3 of them because "They didn't look too good."

Because I was still recovering from my last surgery, my doctor didn't want me to sit in the truck for that long of a distance so I sent my top man Zac. Zac picked up the donkey and I met him at our Vet's office. Little John or LJ, named by Zac on the trip, was only 1-1/2 years old. He was a very sweet little guy with that look of kindness in his eyes. But he also had the unmistakable look of pain.

The "lump" that the farmer had told me about was actually a bone tumor. It engulfed the whole left side of Little John's skull and completely blocked his left nasal passage and was compressing his right side too. We took several x-rays and had three Veterinarians review LJ's case. All three Vets, who I respect greatly, held the same opinion. LJ was in awful pain and there was absolutely nothing we could do for him.

As always, these decisions fall to me alone. I sat with Little John in a little stall at the Vet's office and weighed the facts. As I sat there stroking the little donkey's neck and talked to him about good things I knew in my heart that I needed to provide the only real help that I could give this poor creature. I signed the euthanasia contract and while the Veterinarian administered the drugs, I hugged his neck and hopefully eased his passing.

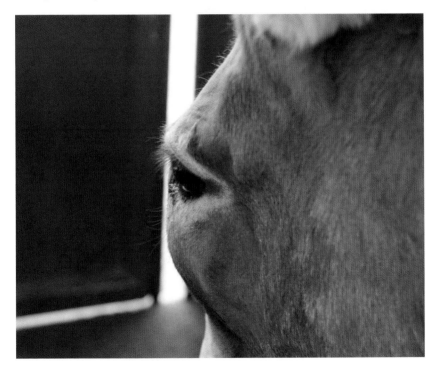

With Little John's story, like so many others... It is what it is. I handled it as best I could and then I prepared myself for the next one. And I didn't have long to wait. On the ride back to the ranch I received a call from my people along the Mexican Border. We had caught a burro that had crossed the Rio Grande from Mexico in one of our traps.

Since Zac had just spent a full day in the truck and I was going a little stir crazy, I decided to make the trip myself. I have absolutely no control over the cancer that keeps coming back but I will not sit around and let it dictate my life. After all...It is what is it.

The little burro that was in my trap wasn't wild as I had expected. He was very domesticated and obviously beaten. He shook uncontrollably when I approached and as I got closer to him I could see all of the open wounds. He had been beaten by someone and severely.

Like Little John, this little fellow was around 1-1/2 years old. But unlike Little John this donkeys eyes did not show kindness, they were filled with terror. He had no trust for people and that is probably why he escaped across the river looking for relief from the horrors of his previous life.

As gently as I could, I loaded the little guy into our trailer. Because he was caught along the border, I had to put him into our special quarantine area and test his blood for anything that he might be carrying. I allowed the little burro a few days to get used to his new surroundings before I started to sit with him.

Mainly I would just sit there and read a book or draw pictures in the dirt, the important thing was for the little burro to see that not all people were bad. While I sat there I also thought a lot about Little John. I started to get caught up in thinking about how unfair things can be. It was unfair that Little John had a tumor and it was unfair that this donkey had to suffer through all of the terrible beatings.

But then I remembered my mantra...It is what it is. I can't help what happened to these donkeys. I can only help them deal with the results.

I decided to name the new burro Little Juan. I think LJ would have appreciated that.

Mean Ass Kulans

Peaceful Valley Donkey Rescue has always tried to stay within the realm of helping donkeys. We have taken in the occasional mule and even some llamas, goats, sheep, cows and pigs...but we TRY to remain faithful to the cause of Donkey Rescue.

Our first experience with an Asian Wild Ass started with a call from a county officer in Kerrville, TX. They had found a donkey roaming the streets and no one had come to claim it. This is not uncommon as PVDR responds to dozens of donkey abandonment cases all across Texas each month.

Upon arrival, we knew immediately that this was no donkey. Its ears were too short and it did not have a cross on its back, only a single strip from mane to the tail. It was also a two-tone color that I had never seen on a donkey. And most importantly, it did not act like a donkey. It was aggressive and dangerous.

We did some research on the ride home and discovered that we had in our possession a Turkmenistan Kulan, a member of the Asian Ass family. As a species they have never been domesticated and from our initial contact it is obvious why: these things are dangerous.

With the help of our donors, we were able to make a safe and secure enclosure for our newest resident and all was wonderful once again, until...

We received another call from another Texas county and this time they had two Kulans, a male and a female. These were in even worse shape than the first one and it was obvious that they had run through fences as they were severely cut up. The female was obviously in the late stages of pregnancy.

We have since solved the mystery of where these Kulans are coming from. Many ranches in Texas offer "canned hunts". People pay thousands of dollars to hunt on these private ranches and shoot all types of exotic and even endangered animals. These Kulans probably escaped from these types of ranches and the reason they went unclaimed is that the ranch owners would face serious fines if their animals were escaping their property.

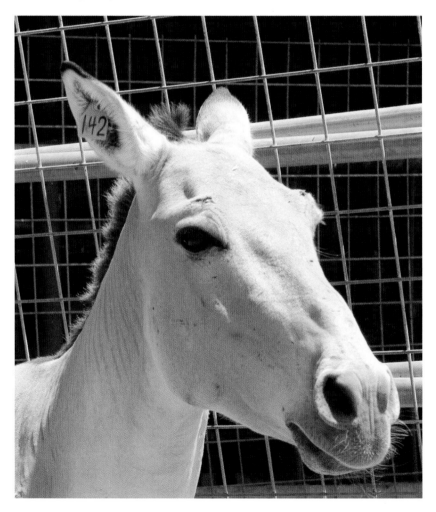

With the birth of K4, born on 08/06/2011, we now have four Kulans at our San Angelo Texas Facility. The males are highly territorial and must be kept separated or they will fight. Because of their speed, ability to jump and wild streak all four Kulans are in a secure area of the ranch. They get very nervous around people so visitors can only few them from a distance. It is our hope to one day build a much larger area for them to roam.

The Asian wild ass subspecies are quite different from the African species. The coat is usually sandy, but varies from reddish grey, fawn, to pale chestnut. The animal possesses an erect, dark mane which runs from the back of the head and along the neck. The mane is then followed by a dark brown stripe running along the back, to the root of the tail.

Of the five subspecies of Equus Hemionus, one is extinct and two are endangered.

About the Author

Mark Meyers is the Executive Director and Co-founder of the Peaceful Valley Donkey Rescue. Mark was born in Leavenworth, Kansas and did most of his growing up in Southern California.

Mark's professional background is in the construction field. Mark was a licensed General Contractor and a licensed Electrical Contractor.

Since founding the Rescue with his wife Amy, Mark has devoted his life to improving the plight of the American Donkey. Closing his businesses in 2005, Mark and Amy went full time into the rescue field.

Mark has written several books and has had innumerable articles published throughout the world. Mark and PVDR have been featured both nationally and internationally in television, documentaries, radio and nearly every major market newspaper in the United States. Mark and Bonney were featured on National Geographic's website.

I would like to remember some friends who we have lost over the last few years.

Chris Lea
August 18, 1967 - September 06, 2010

Chris and I came up in construction together beginning in the mid 1980's. Chris was married to Gina Lea who had a little sister that I was very fond of, so fond that I have been married to her for more than 20 years. Chris was a fellow electrical contractor and more importantly a friend. He left behind his wife Gina, three adult sons and his daughter Trinity. Chris was diagnosed with cancer and died way too soon.

Nathan Meza
June 09, 1992 - July 21, 2009

Nathan lived just down the road from our very first location in Texas. His mother stopped by one day to say that she had a teenage son who needed a job. As I had no help on the ranch I jumped at the chance. Nathan was a great kid and well liked by our whole town. He was always polite and never without a smile. Nathan died from an electrical shock outside of his parent's house.

Chris Hay
May 17, 1979 - November 15, 2006

Chris was an employee of my construction company but more importantly a friend. Chris had the sharpest wit of anyone I had ever met. He was intelligent and talented well beyond his 24 years. Chris was instrumental in the construction and erection (and yes he would have giggled and tried to make me say it again) of many of the buildings at our Tehachapi Facility. Chris died in a automobile accident.

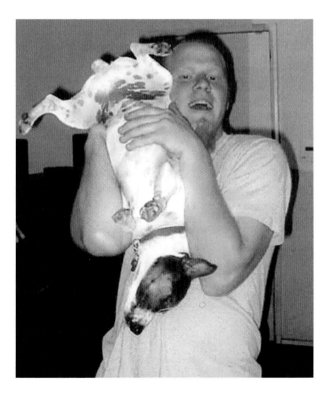

Thanks to the following people for their continued support:

David, Michele & Donna Marie for their work on this book.

Shelly for keeping her kids close to me.

Zac for being one of the sane ones and taking this whole thing seriously.

My mom, well for just being my mom.

Jake and Tovar for being there whenever I need them.

Josh for always making us proud.

Elmer and J.B. for their words of wisdom.

All of the folks who operate our Satellite Adoption Centers.

All of the people who financially support the work of the Rescue.

And my dogs, no matter how many hours in the truck or nights in a hotel I can always count on them 100%.

THE END

PVDR Contact Information:
Peaceful Valley Donkey Rescue
National Operations Center
PO Box 216
Miles, TX 76861

Phone	866-366-5731
Fax	866-898-6182
Web	www.donkeyrescue.org
Email	info@donkeyrescue.org
Facebook	www.facebook.com/peacefulvalleydonkeyrescue
YouTube	www.youtube.com/donkeyrescue
Twitter	@donkeyrescue

Mark Meyers Contact Information
Peaceful Valley Donkey Rescue
Att: Mark Meyers
8317 Duckworth Road
San Angelo, TX 76861

Phone	325-468-4123
Email	mark@donkeyrescue.org
Facebook	www.facebook.com/donkeyrescue
Twitter	@burroman

BürroCøllies Contact Information

Web	www.burrocollies.com
Facebook	www.facebook.com/burro.collies
YouTube	www.youtube.com/burrocollies
Twitter	@burrocollies